Dixie

The [...] b [...] in

and please [...] my Prayers – I pray God surrounds you and you start being stronger every day – You have always been strong – I remember you in school as being outgoing, fun loving and someone who knew what she wanted – married her class sweetheart and raised a family – You and Connie were quite a team a lot of girls looked up to you – Such the memories Dixie, I hope I can come see you when I get in town the end of May – I wish you well, lots of Prayers and thanks for the memories – God Bless you and your family –

God Bless
Marlene Scott
2016

God
Inspired *The*
Best *in* Me
Yes God Spoke I wrote

MARLENE WHEELER SCOTT

authorHOUSE®

AuthorHouse™
1663 Liberty Drive
Bloomington, IN 47403
www.authorhouse.com
Phone: 1 (800) 839-8640

© 2016 Marlene Wheeler Scott. All rights reserved.

No part of this book may be reproduced, stored in a retrieval system, or
transmitted by any means without the written permission of the author.

Published by AuthorHouse 01/30/2016

ISBN: 978-1-5049-6788-4 (sc)
ISBN: 978-1-5049-6789-1 (e)

Print information available on the last page.

Any people depicted in stock imagery provided by Thinkstock are models,
and such images are being used for illustrative purposes only.
Certain stock imagery © Thinkstock.

This book is printed on acid-free paper.

Because of the dynamic nature of the Internet, any web addresses or links contained in
this book may have changed since publication and may no longer be valid. The views
expressed in this work are solely those of the author and do not necessarily reflect the
views of the publisher, and the publisher hereby disclaims any responsibility for them.

My Introduction

My name is Marlene Wheeler Scott and I live in Santee, S.C. I was born in Kentucky, but I grew up and graduated in a little farming town called Camden, Ohio... After graduation joined the Navy where I met and married My husband, also in the U.S.N., living mostly in Charleston, S.C.... We had four children, three sons and a daughter, nine grandchildren and six great grandchildren and we have been married for fifty six years My second son, Mark, passed away suddenly and unexpectedly leaving a deep void in so many of our lives, especially in mine as I thought my life too had ended... I started writing to him after he passed, talking to him, asking him questions, all in poem that came from my heart of how I felt, how I thought he had felt, and even to things I felt he would have said to me and his loved ones.. Writing seemed to bring me closer to him and gave me more of an understanding about how precious life is and I became more aware that the time God gives us with our loved ones is indeed God's gift to us and we should give thanks to God every day for that Blessing A few months after his passing, we moved to a small town, Santee, S.C. where I met a friend, Shirley Mcleod who took me to this small church on the lake, Lakeside Outreach Ministries where I found love, peace and understanding and God...

I soon met others with pain and suffering from the loss of loved ones, who also was looking for answers... It was then I truly began writing I began writing poems for others who had experienced the loss of a loved one, or was having spiritual, emotional, or health problems... my poems seemed to connect with them, giving them peace and understanding, sometimes, it was as if their loved ones were giving me words to write and give to their loved ones here and my writing for them also brought me closer to my son.... God showed me that death does not separate us, it brings us closer together.... I know without God, my family and my church, my poems would never have been, for it was God who gave me these words..... God showed me the impact words written can have and because of the power of words however they are used, words of comfort, compassion, support and understanding to one another, they must be used with wisdom.. God kept His Word... let us now keep ours

Marlene Wheeler Scott

About the Author

My name is Marlene Wheeler Scott and I live in Santee, S.C. I was born in Kentucky, but I grew up and graduated in a little farming town called Camden, Ohio... After graduation joined the Navy where I met and married My husband, also in the U.S.N., living mostly in Charleston, S.C.... We had four children, three sons and a daughter, nine grandchildren and six great grandchildren and we have been married for fifty six years My second son, Mark, passed away suddenly and unexpectedly leaving a deep void in so many of our lives, especially in mine as I thought my life too had ended... I started writing to him after he passed, talking to him, asking him questions, all in poem that came from my heart of how I felt, how I thought he had felt, and even to things I felt he would have said to me and his loved ones.. Writing seemed to bring me closer to him and gave me more of an understanding about how precious life is and I became more aware that the time God gives us with our loved ones is indeed God's gift to us and we should give thanks to God every day for that Blessing A few months after his passing, we moved to a small town, Santee, S.C. where I met a friend, Shirley Mcleod who took me to this small church on the lake, Lakeside Outreach Ministries where I found love, peace and understanding and God...

I soon met others with pain and suffering from the loss of loved ones, who also was looking for answers... It was then I truly began writing I began writing poems for others who had experienced the loss of a loved one, or was having spiritual, emotional, or health problems... my poems seemed to connect with them, giving them peace and understanding, sometimes, it was as if their loved ones were giving me words to write and give to their loved ones here and my writing for them also brought me closer to my son.... God showed me that death does not separate us, it brings us closer together.... I know without God, my family and my church, my poems would never have been, for it was God who gave me these words..... God showed me the impact words written can have and because of the power of words however they are used, words of comfort, compassion, support to and for one another, they must be used with wisdom and understanding.... God kept His promise and His word to us, let us now keep our love and our word to our fellow man

Marlene Wheeler Scott

Dedication

Thank You God

I am dedicating the writings of my book to my beloved brother, Garry Lee Wheeler Garry Lee was the 9th of 10 children in our family....He was the youngest of five brothers, and he was the 3rd brother to pass away... He now will be with his two other brothers, Ray Earl, 3 days old and Avery Jordon, age 15 years.

My brother Garry Lee was born about two years before I graduated from High School, and then, I joined the Navy, moved away from home, married a man in the Navy and moved around with him and began my own family, so, I did not get to see him in his early childhood, or see him graduate and I truly feel that I missed out on so much of his life.... He was what we five older children called, the second half of the family...so, I missed out on the childhood of the second half.

Garry Lee graduated, went into the Army, following in the footsteps of his two older brothers, Roy and Jerry.... He served his time, got out and returned home where he began work for a company called Staff Market where he worked for 29 years and I must say that no amount of words can say enough about this wonderful company and what they did for him when he became so ill.... From all his family, we say, 'thank you'..he loved you and the thought of you as family... He was not married, no children, so he dedicated his life to his work, his beloved Mother and all his brothers and sisters and their families.

Garry Lee loved his Mother and loved being with her and doing things with her... he would take her out to eat, go over and play her favorite games with her, and go with her to church on Sunday... they were very close, and he was devastated when she passed away three years ago... Shortly there after, he was told that he had Cancer.. The Cancer became his biggest challenge in life.... It became a fight that would eventually be the death of him, but, he never lost his Faith and he never gave up.... He lost this battle of Cancer on Sunday, Sept. 20, 2015.... He would have been 64 on Sept. 29... Garry Lee is now in God's Hands and in the arms of his beloved Mother.

Garry Lee was a strong, caring young man, hard working and he loved his family, I thank God I was able to be a part of his adult life to be able to do many things with him... He had many family gatherings, cookouts, and reunions at his home, I referred to it as the Family Retreat, we all loved to go there... We were and we still are a very close knit family

I am so proud to call him my brother, and so proud to be called his 'big sister'... My heart aches that I was not able to have spent more time with him and to store up more memories of his younger years

I was able to make two trips to Ohio to be by his side while he was in the hospital before his passing... although he was in so much pain, could not talk, he communicated with all of us, making us really learn lip reading and be still kept his humor and even his concern about his brothers and sisters.... told him in the hospital that I was going to dedicate my book I was writing to him, he smiled and mouthed the words, "now you want to make me famous", squeezed my hand and smiled again.

Yes, Garry Lee, responding to your comment, you will always be 'famous' in my eyes, all our eyes, for you will live forever in our hearts and because of you, our lives were and will be forever blessed.... You are the STAR and will always be a STAR, and now when we go outside at night and look up into the Sky, we will see this Star, shining so brightly and twinkling as if to say to us, "Here I am, high in the Sky.... I never said good bye"

Garry Lee, my youngest brother, my wonderful brother, I love you/we love you... you were the bright spot in all our lives.... God hold you, keep you until we can all be together again.

Garry Lee Wheeler
Sept. 29, 1951-Sept. 20Th, 20151951-Sept. 20Th, 2015

Mr. Rooster

I keep remembering the strangest thing that I had ever seen, that happened when I was a little boy

I grew up on a farm where we had a large hen house, and it was my job to go there every day and collect the eggs from the hen's nests, but, I had missed one day, and when I went into the hen house the next day, in one corner of the hen house was a gathering of many eggs, but, not with the hen sitting on them, but a Rooster…He was sitting on those eggs

and no matter how hard I tried, he would not come off that nest and give up those eggs

Now, how was I going to explain to my Uncle Mark and Aunt Patti that there would be no fresh eggs today for Grandma to fix breakfast, and then have to tell them the reason why….Well, I did try to explain and after they had their good laugh, they followed me outside to the hen house to see for themselves… Sure enough, there was Mr. Rooster sitting on the pile of eggs and he acted like it was completely natural for him to be there

They both burst out laughing again, then, my Uncle Mark said, "now that looks like a match, made straight out of Heaven"…I did not completely understand what he meant, but, I guess he meant that if that if God intended this to happen, then, happen it would be

I was told that a hen usually sits on her eggs for twenty-one days before they hatched, but my Uncle Mark said, he believed that Rooster was going to sit on those eggs for as long as it took for them to be hatch, then laughed and said he thought the Rooster would make a great 'Mother and Father"

Well, the day finally came when the eggs hatched and everyone just shook their heads in utter astonishment as they watched all those little chicks following Mr. Rooster around ..This rooster definitely had something to 'CROW' about now...Mr. Rooster felt like he had been chosen and called upon to protect something and he succeeded against all the odds and yes, many doubts

I have to say that, that summer so long ago proved to be, not only unusual, but, a learning experience for me for it taught me to never give up in life if there was something I wanted to do, I could do it....What a wonderful memory I have of my childhood because of Mr. Rooster

MORAL of this story: Any Challenge won
is something to CROW about

Marlene Wheeler Scott

The Boy Who Never Laughed

Once upon a time, in the year 2000 B.C....there came to the town square a circus, and with the circus were clowns who could and did make people forget about their worries for awhile by making them laugh, but, there was one man who would not laugh

This young man married and had a son of his own, named him Grayson, but, he still never found anything to laugh about, so his son Grayson never learned to laugh either because he never seen or heard laughter around the house

One day Grayson heard that there was a circus coming to town and he had never been to a circus, all his friends, were so excited about it and when they told

Grayson about the circus Grayson asked them "just what is a circus?" they told him that it was a circus with a large tent and that it had lots and lots of clowns and lions and elephants who did many tricks and would make you laugh

Grayson went home and told his Dad about this thing called a circus and asked him if he would take him to the circus..... His Dad told him yes, and Grayson got very excited

The big day came and Grayson and his Dad went to the circus and they sat together on the very bottom row so they could get a good look at the clowns....Then, when the clowns came out doing their tricks, everybody started clapping and laughing.... Grayson's Dad just sat there, not smiling, then a clown came dancing over, stood in front of them and started juggling and dancing and all of a sudden, Grayson's Dad started laughing and he laughed so hard that he fell off the front row onto the ground, rolling in laughter...Grayson watched his Dad and suddenly, he too broke out into laughter

They could not stop laughing and they laughed all the way home Grayson and his Dad really enjoyed their day together and they went home knowing that every day thereafter would be brighter because it would be filled with laughter

Moral of this story:......
A clown can overcome every frown
Laughter will turn your life around
If you wear a frown, turn it upside down
Because laughter is what makes the world go round

Reading of the Bible

Once upon a time, there was a young boy named Terry, who loved to read, He had begun to read at a very early age....His Mother Bettielee told him that she too loved to read and that she especially loved reading the bible, together, they began to read, she would read to him and then let him read some of the bible to her

Terry, though he was very young, began reading the bible by himself, even though many of the words he did not, as yet understand, but he really loved reading the stories in the bible, such as Noah's Ark, the big flood, the beginning of man, the committment of the first sin, and of the creation by God of the earth and everything on it in six days, then, gave us one day to rest, making it a week....The stories of Jesus, and the end of time to come....He loved reading and absorbed everything that was in the bible.. He came to identify with the Bible as the book of Truth and Predictions of things to come to past

Since he too was still a child, he especially loved reading about how Jesus loved the little children so much.. He knew Jesus loved him too, because the bible told him so

It saddened him when he read how Jesus had to die on the cross on Calvary Hill, but did it because He wanted to save His children from a world of sin and to let them know that He would not die, but would arise again and ascend to Heaven where He would sit on the right hand of God, the Father Almighty

Terry, at his young age, asked Jesus to come into his heart so that he too could be saved from the wages of sin...He told Jesus that he wanted to go out and spread His word to all he could reach...he said he wanted to become a Preacher

Terry did become a Preacher, though it was many years later, but he lived for God and lived God's word and went out to share and to spread God's Words, the truth, that in the Bible you will find the truth, the peace, the comfort and the answers that we all seek

THE BIBLE: Read it....Love it...Keep it in your heart forever

Today...I Just Wanted

When Blake opened his eyes and got out of bed
He already had plans for the day in his head
I just want to go and play outside
Maybe get on my bike and go for a nice little ride
Maybe even ride my little skateboard
So many choices, I know I will not get bored

Maybe even go to the beach today
Where I can build sandcastles, run and play
Taking my kite to fly at the beach
Watching it fly as high as it will reach

But, all of sudden it began to rain and to Blake's sorrow
He said, I will just stay home and try again tomorrow

Today, these things that I was planning to do
Will have to be put on hold for a day or two
But, I will find lots to do around the house
I promise my Mother, I will be quiet as a mouse
Even my sister Brianna, I promise not to tease

Maybe once in a while, I'll steal a little squeeze
Then come bedtime, with my family I will share
My love for them, as my Daddy hears my Prayer

The Moral of this story is:...Sometimes in life, self made plans do not always work out the way we want them to, so, we must accept them, make the most of what we have now and what we can do and TRY AGAIN

Yassee

This is the story of a young boy, Johnny
and his beloved and very loyal dog, Yassee

Johnny lived in a home that was surrounded by a lot of yard, property.... He would go out and look at all the space and wish that he had someone or something he could share it with...Johnny walked around throwing stones, sticks, kicking at things, he just seemed so lonely...

One day, his Mother was looking out the window and was watching Johnny, just seeming lost and trying to find something to do, so, she called Johnny into the house and said, "Johnny, would you be happy if you had a puppy"? Johnny's eyes lit up and, jumping up he said, "oh yes Mother, can we go get one now"? His Mother said yes and they went out and got into the car and drove around to several SPCA and Dog Kennels...The third one they came to, Johnny seen this little puppy that was wagging his tail, bobbing his head up and down, and his soft little barks sounded like they were asking Johnny to take him home and that is what Johnny did

Johnny was so happy, his Mother had never seen him so happy...Johnny and Yassee became inseparable, they went every where together and did every thing together...They would go in the yard and Yassee and Johnny would romp around on the ground, he would bring back sticks and balls that Johnny would throw, and even played in the creek together.... At night when Johnny would go to bed, Yassee would lay on the floor beside him...Johnny knew he was safe with Yassee beside him

In the morning when Johnny left to go to school, Yassee would walk with him to the bus, watch him get on, then, when it was time for Johnny to come home from school, Yassee was always right there waiting for him....the other children had come to know Yassee too and they would yell, "Hi Yassee", and Yassee would wag his tail as if to say "hi" to the kids on the bus

One day, when Johnny got off the bus, Yassee was not there, the kids all yelled, "where is Yassee today"? Johnny knew something was wrong and he began crying and ran home.....He ran into the house yelling, "Mother, where is Yassee, what is wrong?'

His Mother hugged him and told him that Yassee had become sick and she had taken him to the Vet.....Johnny said, "Mother, can you take me to the Vet, where he is at and see if I can see Yassee?....Yes, said his Mother, and they both got into the car and went to the Vet Clinic where Yassee was being treated....When they got there, Johnny ran in and ask the Vet Dr. if he could see his dog and the the Vet Dr. said yes

The Vet Dr. took Johnny into this little room and there on the table lay his beloved dog, Yassee...Yassee was very weak, but, when he seen Johnny, he slowly raised his head and even wagged his tail...Johnny and his dog were so close that Johnny just knew Yassee was waiting for him and was not going to leave him without saying good-bye

Johnny then asked the Vet Dr. if he could hold Yassee and the Vet Dr. said yes, got a blanket, put it in Johnny's lap then picked up the dog and laid him in his lap....They sat there together for about an hour, Johnny was talking to him, rubbing his head and reaching down from time to time to kiss him on his face....He was remembering their times together....Yassee seemed to understand, he raised his head, looked at

God Inspired The Best in Me   9

Johnny, wagged his tail once, licked his face, then his body went limp.... Johnny said that he felt Yassee held on til they could see each other one more time....Johnny said, "Yassee was a part of me, my friend, my companion, he was a part of my heart and will forever be

The OOZ-Formula for Life

Once upon a time, there was a man named Randall who lived in a very old and remote Castle...He and his wife were loners and did not get many visitors One day he heard a knock at the door of his castle and when he got to the door and opened it, there stood a witch, however, he did not know that she was a witch

She asked him if she could please have a bite to eat, because she has not eaten in several days, but Randall started laughing at her and slammed the door in her face

He went back into the big dining room inside his castle, and just as he sat down and started eating, he heard the door bell ring, going, Ding-Dong, so, Randall got up, opened the door yelling, "what"???? He then heard the witch say, "wink a dink—wink a dong, I am turning you into a Dragon, you will be cursed until you can find the formula of life, OOZ, then, and only then can you have your life back...You will become old and tired and first your body, then your head will turn into a Dragon's head...Randall slammed the door in her face again, ran into the living room screaming for his wife

He remained in his castle and over the years, he became old and tired and true to the witch's curse, his body was beginning to turn into a Dragon and he was trying to hide it from everyone by changing and putting on different articles of clothing

God Inspired The Best in Me

One day he yelled, I cannot take this any longer, if I do
not find the OOZ-FORMULA of Life, I will never be
a man again, but doomed for life to be a Dragon

Randall ran outside, jumped into his Royal Dodge Viper and drove
120 miles an hour into town...When he got into town, he went from
store to store trying on clothes and costumes or whatever he could
hide his body in....The last store he went into, he was trying on some
clothes and he turned to look in the rear view mirror to see his image
and there, beside inside the mirror was the OOZ-FORMULA...
Randall grabbed the mirror and ran as fast as he could back home

I finally have it he yelled to his wife ...now I can be a man again....so,
he found a rock and he broke the mirror over the rock, thus breaking
the Witch's spell....Suddenly, he started turning back into a man.....

Yes, he had found the meaning of NICE and he
had been given a second chance at life

Moral of this story:

We should treat people right...we all make mistakes,
and sometimes, some of us are given a 2nd chance to
learn from our mistakes and to make amends

Do Unto Others as you would have them Do Unto You

Marlene Wheeler Scott

Mr. Rooster vs Mr. Fox

Little Red Rooster, just what are you going to do
When that old mean Fox comes looking for you
Are you just going to strut around the farm all day long
Crowing and strutting and acting like you are strong?

Or, will you dare him to come onto your domain
Telling Mr. Fox, you are not leaving, that here you will remain?
Yes, the Sly Fox may think that he is smarter than you
But, he has not seen just what you can do

For when you sound the alarm with your famous crow
Then the farmer will know
That with his shotgun, he will come a gunning
And that Sly old Fox will start running

So, Mr. Fox, you better stay away from me
Or you will soon become history.

Yes, the Fox may have been sly, but, he did not know
The power Mr. Rooster had when he crowed.

Tiffany's Song

Tiffany knew she was going to be very busy this week....
She was also very nervous and excited because she had been
asked to sing a song in church next Sunday morning....

"What will I sing"? Tiffany asked herself because she knew she
was going to have to practice..Tiffany loved her church and
singing on Sundays...Tiffany was truly a child of God's

Tiffany went around the house all week singing different songs..
What a job it was going to be to pick one because she loved
them all, so when she went to bed that night, Tiffany got down
on her knees to say her prayers, and tonight she had a special
request...She ask God if He would pick the song for her to sing

The next night as she was getting ready for bed, she turned on her
bedroom light only to find out that the light was out, so, she went
into the kitchen to get a flashlight...As she was shining the flashlight
around her room, she suddenly cried out... "that's it"...this is the
answer to my Prayer...I now know what I will sing next Sunday..

When Sunday morning came, Tiffany was up bright and
early and so excited....She kept practicing her song as she was
getting ready for church.....She put on her prettiest dress

She could not wait for her and her family to get to church

When it was time for her to sing, Tiffany got up, looked around, then smiled and said, "I am dedicating this song to God because He chose it for me", then she sang THIS LITTLE LIGHT of MINE.... She sang it beautifully and everyone clapped, then she was asked if she would sing again next Sunday and Tiffany smiled and said yes, because she knew God would help her pick out a special song to sing

The Fancy Donkey

This is the story of a donkey who thought she was better than all the other donkey's and said that she was going to be famous one day

The farmer had given each of his donkey's a name, just because he enjoyed calling them out by name and watch them come to him...they all, in his words knew who they were and always ready to do whatever work he had for them to do...On the other hand, there was one donkey, her name was Nancy and she did not want to work or earn her keep.... She would just walk around in the fields, pretending she was working, but, just looking for something to do besides work

One day while Nancy was in the field walking around, she suddenly stopped ...she saw something lying in the field and went over to check it out and she brayed out loudly, "it's a woman's' hat", then she reached down and put it on top of her head...She began to strut around and she kept saying, "look at me, I am beautiful, I look so fancy in this beautiful hat".

Well, when the other animals heard about Nancy, the donkey who was so fancy, the word really got around and people from every town started coming to see this special donkey who was now so famous because of a hat she found and made her so Fancy

Yes, she became so famous that the farmer decided that she did not have to work like the other donkeys to earn her keep, because she had also made his farm famous and he was enjoying all the company and excitement....So, when you pass a farm with lots of donkeys in the field....look closely, because you will see the donkey that they call Nancy, strutting around in her new found straw hat that on her looked so fancy

Dragon Hunt

Once upon a time, there was a WIZARD and he liked Dragons and he had one, but, then he heard that the King had put up a $2000.00 reward and the promise that whoever brought him the head of a Dragon he would make them a Knight, so, everybody took up arms, ran out into the forest, and so began the Dragon Hunt

The Wizard got scared, so, he took his Dragon to this little hole in the ground inside a cave and he took his Dragon into the cave, and tried to squeeze him into this deep hole, but the Dragon got out of the hole and it was so big, that it is now known as the Grand Canyon, but the Dragon remained in the cave

Everyone was still looking for the Dragon and it took them one year and three months to find the cave the Dragon was living in, and when they approached the cave, they sent their whole Army into the cave where a fierce battle was fought, all the Army was killed and the Dragon won

When the Kingdom heard of this, they dethroned their King and elected a new King....This King liked Dragons and wanted his people to be friends with the Dragons and if they wanted them as pets, so be it

So, the King, his kingdom and all the Dragons became friends and there was peace in the Kingdom

The moral of this story is that, even if someone or something is different than you, if you will take the time to understand them, be nice to them, treat them with respect, that there will be peace among all

Trigger

Once upon a time, there was a black and white pony called Trigger... He lived in a barn on a dusty old road that led to Old Mill Pond..... It was completely fenced in, but, never did Trigger think of jumping the fence and running away for he was very happy here

Trigger was a very gentle pony who loved children....he did not have a mean bone in his body...The highlight of his day was when his owner, Mr. Jim would let the children come to pet him and ride them around...he also loved pulling them in the cart around the farm and giving them a tour of where he lived

Trigger had a really unusual habit though...he loved eating scraps from restaurants, like apple peels and cores, and his favorite, Banana Pudding, so, the children knew to bring him these treats when they came over and Trigger looked forward to their visits

Trigger was so gentle with the children, that when they were riding on his back, and he would feel a fly land on his back, he would not even swish his tail to get it off for fear of hitting the children...This pony would literally give his life for a child

One day, a lot of children had come to the barn yard to ride the horses and the pony, so, Mr. Jim placed one of the children on another horse in the barnyard, it was a large thoroughbred horse, and as soon as he did, the thoroughbred started bucking, throwing the child off his back, and then he tried to trample on her, but, Trigger, seeing all this, ran between the frightened child and the thoroughbred horse, protecting her and daring the horse to try and harm her

Yes, Trigger became a hero that day and word of what he had done spread throughout the town and people began coming from all around to see this ever so gentle pony...Trigger became known as a symbol of gentleness and bravery and would change forever, the way people thought of little ponies

Trigger ….this gentle pony, was called the Angel in the Animal World that watches over ALL the children of the world`

The Alphabet...A To Z

Here are some animals, starting from A to Z
Describing them for you to read and see
That every word however, either by you or me
Contains a letter in the Alphabet, from A to Z

ALLIGATORS...Very dangerous, stay away from them please
BIRDS...Always cheerful, chirping, flying in the sky so free
CATS...Purrs so quietly, are cuddly, makes a wonderful pet
DOGS...Protective of your home, friendly, you they never forget

ELEPHANTS...Huge...has a long nose they call a trunk
FROGS...Croaks a lot, likes water and sitting on logs or stumps
GIRAFFES..Very long neck, long legs, making them very tall
HORSES...Used as transportation, but
known as a Champion Racer to all
IQUANNA....He is so ugly, better looking I know he wants to be
JELLYFISH...They are transparent and they live in the sea

KANGAROOS...They have pouches to
carry their young and they hop
LEOPARDS...Wow....fast and beautiful, but hunted a lot
MOUSE....Can be problem, their favorite food is cheese
NEWTS...Little boys love to catch and play with these
OWLS..When he hoots, you will know he is around
PIGS...They love to wallow in the muddy ground

QUAILS...A hunter's delight, there is no doubt
RHINOS...A dangerous horn that they call his snout
SNAKES....They hiss and slither in the grass
TURTLES...They go so slow, in a race they would finish last
UNICORNS....He has a horn in the middle of his forehead
VULTURES....They live off animals and things that are dead

WHALES....They live in the Oceans and Sea, called our biggest fish
X-RAYS...Sees through things, good results is everyone's wish
YAKS..A cousin of the Moose because they look so much alike
ZEBRAS....Has a striped body, but, are they black or are they white?

God Inspired The Best in Me

A Week In the Life of Abbi

Good morning Mom and Dad! "This is going to be a really great week...I am going to eat a big breakfast this morning, because I have a really big day at school.. "What is so exciting about today?", asked her Mother, saying that most kids hate Monday mornings.... "Oh no" said Abbi.... just listen to my schedule"

MONDAY: Today we are doing a big Science Project at school and you know I love working on Science Projects....trying to invent new things was always exciting and a challenge to her..... Then in the Art Department, we are working on drawing a Wall Murial....I love doing this and I am so excited to get started... Abbi loved doing things that she felt would help or make others happy

TUESDAY: This was another favorite and looked for day... Abbi would be going for her piano lessons...Abbi loved to play the piano and sing, she called it one of her favorite past times, she would learn new songs to sing in Church

WEDNESDAY: Abbi would now go to the Gym as she does every Wednesday during her recess time at school where she would practice basketball with some of her friends... She was in hopes that she would be able to play on the All Girls Basketball Team and she also knew that in order to make the team, she had to really practice

THURSDAY: Today she goes to the Animal Shelter after school to see what new animals had arrived, then she would help feed them, and also walk the dogs....Abbi loved animals and this was her way of being able to stay close to all the animals and to help out at the Animal Shelter... "I might decide to become a Vet one day", said Abbi

FRIDAY: !WOW! This week sure flew by fast....school is out and now, this was the day she gets to spend with her Mother, in the kitchen and to help her fix supper...Abbi would fix her favorite food for supper and looked forward to spending it with her Mother and Father.....It was also the last night of school, and after supper, she would get to go for a ride with her dad on his motorcycle..She loved this time with her Father

SATURDAY: This day was very special to Abbi also, but, this one held a special place in her heart..Abbi was born with a Birthmark on the side of her face/mouth, but, thanks to V.B.M., they were able to help Abbi with her surgery and much more....Abbi was chosen as a Poster Child for V.B.M and Abbi wanted to give back as much of herself and the awareness of others as she could, so she would go out and do whatever she could to help raise monies and awareness for V.B.M., selling cookies, washing cars, passing out posters, whatever she could do, she was available...ABBI IS A SPECIAL PERSON

SUNDAY: Now, this truly is her favorite day, for it is the day she and her family are all together, going to church and getting to sing and to praise God and give Him thanks for all His blessings.... Abbi said, "Mother, I love every day of the week that God gives me, but, each day is different and I feel like one of the luckiest kids alive for God has given to me a wonderful Mother, Father and my beautiful, wonderful sister, Amanda..I look forward to every day of every week and the unexpected new adventures it brings

God Inspired The Best in Me

The Mountain Versus the Squirrel

Mr. Squirrel was out one day running, climbing the trees and the mountains, just wanting to have fun, when suddenly, Mr. Squirrel heard an angry voice roaring down upon him saying, "what are you doing here in my space?"

The mountain and Mr. Squirrel had a few words and then a terrible argument Mr. Squirrel tried to explain that he was just having fun and loved running in the wide open spaces, but the mountain roared back, "well, you cannot because everything here belongs to me, including the trees and even the gentle breeze, and since I am bigger than you, you have to go"

Mr. Squirrel then stood up, swished his tail around, chattered a little, then said, "well, you can have your space, the trees and the breeze, but, you have to stay here forever, you cannot leave, but, I can go anytime to anywhere I please because I am free, and yes, you may be bigger than me, but I am stronger
I CAN CRACK A NUT, CAN YOU?"

Moral:
You cannot intrude on others space, but, the air is free, you can always be strong as long as you believe Take nothing from someone but know too Let no one take away from you.

Marlene Wheeler Scott

All Alone and By Myself

As I sit here, all alone, again tonight
Something just does not feel right
I feel warm and cozy beside this glowing fire
I thought being alone was really my desire
I just wanted to have peace and a little quiet
Just once, I thought I would try it
But being alone is not what I expected it to be
The only one I can talk to is ME_ME_ME
So, I'm picking up this telephone
Giving someone a call, please come over, I'm all alone
I'll keep the fire burning, all aglow
So hurry on over, I'm waiting, don't be slow
You're here already, now things feel right
Thanks for coming, I needed the company tonight

An Anguished Prayer

Lord, you have laid upon me such a heavy load
And I find myself walking down a long and rocky road
But every time I thought the end was in sight
I began to stumble, wanting to give up the fight

But then I would then hear Your soft and gentle voice
Saying, "it is now your time, you have to make a choice"
You can lay there weakened, without hope, be in despair
Letting the Devil win by telling you that no one cared

Or you can get up, take My Hand and stand tall
Believing that with Me beside you you will not fall
For I will show you the light at the end of the road
And I will lift from you this heavy load

Yes, sometimes the road is long, but there is an end
Where you will find a renewal of life at the Rivers Bend
For once you travel this road others will follow unafraid
Like Me, they will know the sacrifice for them you too have made

Yes, I have let you walk the road and I have showed you the light
So that you may guide others, giving to them an insight
That if they too want to make Heaven their home
They must travel that road, with Me your will never be alone

So give Me your burdens, reach for and hold my hand
And I will lead you to the Promised Land
No more pain or sorrow or darkness of night
For I will carry your load and show you the light

An Open Line

WHEN I AWAKE HEARING THE BIRDS ALL SINGING
I KNOW IT IS GOD SAYING, "WAKE
UP, YOUR PHONE IS RINGING:
I AM CALLING YOU TO SAY, "I LOVE
YOU AND TO LET YOU KNOW
I WILL BE WITH YOU ALWAYS,
WHEREVER YOU MAY GO"
I'LL HOLD YOUR HAND AND GUIDE YOU THROUGH
WHEREVER YOU GO, WHATEVER YOU DECIDE TO DO
YOU HAVE A DIRECT LINE TO ME, IT IS CALLED <u>PRAYER</u>
JUST USE IT, ANYTIME OR ANYWHERE
YOU WILL NEVER GET A BUSY OR
AN ANSWERING MACHINE
SAYING LEAVE A MESSAGE, I AM
AWAY FOR THE TIME BEING
I ANSWER ALL MY PRAYER CALLS, ONE ON ONE
I AM ON CALL, 24-7, MY WORK IS NEVER DONE

Beautiful Lady

Such a beautiful lady, such a beautiful smile
Always willing to go that extra mile
She will always listen, care and be concerned
While telling us that some things in time we would learn
But she would listen then tell us to do our best
To put our trust in God, He would do the rest
She said in this world in which we now live
We must also learn to forget and to forgive
What a wonderful lady, who has God's special touch
HAPPY BIRTHDAY MS. JANE, WE ALL
LOVE YOU VERY MUCH

THIS WOMAN INDEED IS BEAUTIFUL, SHE HAS MS
AND IS WHEELCHAIR BOUND, BUT, SHE IS ALWAYS
SIMILING AND I HAVE NEVER HEARD HER COMPLAIN,
WHEN I SEE AND TALK TO HER, SHE MAKES MY DAY
AND I AM SO BLESSED TO HAVE COME TO KNOW HER

WRITTEN FOR A SPECIAL LADY THAT I HAVE
BEEN BLESSED TO COME TO KNOW
I ALWAYS SEE A SMILE ON HER FACE NO MATTER
WHAT …SHE IS A BLESSING TO HER FAMILY
AND ALL HER FRIENDS…GOD BLESS
YOU ALWAYS, MS. JANE

Because I Let God In

This morning I awoke with great anticipation
I was waiting to get out of my bed
I no longer was afraid of any temptation
Because I knew God was with me on the road ahead

Somehow I just knew that on the darkest day
The Sun, most surely would shine
I only needed to let God lead the way
I knew God was more than just a friend of mine

God has never left me He is always by my side
He has always filled my empty heart
So today, I knew my prayer would not be denied
As I cried out, "oh God, how great Thou art"

Today God has sent me on a path
That will indeed, change the rest of my life
I will meet a friend who will again make me laugh
Someone who will help me forget my pain and strife

God, I give thanks and praise to you every day
For your love and for filling my empty heart
I now know if you do not let God in, or open that door
You will never find the peace and love that you are searching for

Marlene Wheeler Scott

Beware of Unwanted Love

You told me that you loved me and you cared
But, whenever I needed you, you were never there
Yes, you said if I really loved you
Then I should do whatever you wanted me to do
Yes, flowers to me you would sometime send
But, I soon found out it was all pretend
I was blinded, because I really did love you
And I thought all the while that you loved me too
I even shared with you my love, my secrets, gave you my trust
Because you said my sharing with you was a must
I now know my love for you was real, but yours was not
From our experience, I have truly learned a lot
I cannot lie my heart is aching, for it has truly been broken
But in time it will heal and to you these words I now have spoken
You go your way, I will go mine, but ladies be aware
Do not give your love freely until they show they truly care

Bonita/Crystle

Hello girls, I know it has been a long time
But, I know I am still very much on your mind
Know that I am still watching over all of you
And God is also keeping a record of all you do
Earl my son has sent left to come be with me
He said this was where God now wanted him to be
Tell Raven that her memories of me keeps us close and in touch
And that I love her very, very much
Keri my precious, there are good things for you waiting
But, it is you that just keeps hesitating
You must grab hold, your future must go on
You cannot give up on life and say, it's over and you're done
God says that if we just believe
Blessings from Him, we will receive
Crystle, such a hard worker, holding the family together
Your nieces and nephews think of you as a
friend, their Aunt, their Mother
With two beautiful daughters, your heart they both have won
Your life with them has just begun
Bonita, I now know God had chosen you to be
A preachers' wife, working for his ministry
And if you could only see what God has in store
You would be knocking harder at God's door
I saw what happened to Kevin that day
Bonita, I ask God to let you hear what I am going to say
Man thinks he has plenty of time, God says, "not so"
Only He knows when it is time for man to go

Marlene Wheeler Scott

So it was on that fateful day
It was God, not you who caused Kevin to go away
Sometimes we must all carry our burden throughout the years
When we will question God and cry many tears
God says trials we must sometime endure, before on Him we call
But, He will hold our hand, He will not let us fall
I have seen all of you walking with God, then stumble a bit
But held on to you, saying, "no, not yet"
Your Faith walk with God has now become stronger
And your fear of falling is no longer
To all my grandsons, Corey, Dustin, John and Duane
Your future is your making, no wrong turns, stay in God's lane
My granddaughters, Raven and Keri, you make quite a team
Little spats here and there, but not as bad as they seem
If one needed help, the other would be right there
You are sisters, loving sisters who really care
Kenny, your struggles have been many and long
But, it is your faith that have kept you and your family strong
Thank you all for being my wonderful family
By the way, I see it has increased by three
Always by your side…love you

Brianna

Golly gee, you are growing up way too fast
I want to keep you a little girl, as long as it will last
I want to see you run and play, being a playmate
To all your friends and with your brother Blake
You are such a cheerful, loving child, yes, you are
And you are wiser than your age, oh yes, by far
God made you special then gave you to us
Knowing the love you would give to all you would touch
You have a Mommy and Daddy that loves you so
Every day is a Blessing, as we watch you grow
Grandmas, Grandpa's, aunts, nieces, cousins, just to name a few
That love you so much and will always be here for you
You have a MEME, she is one of a kind
The two of you have a special bind
Today, we have all gathered to help you celebrate and to say
We love you Brianna, have a HAPPY, HAPPY BIRTHDAY

Brothers-Bonded Forever

This is a story about two young brothers, ages six and eight, who are very close to each other.....They do what all little boys like to do..... they play ball, sports, go fishing, ride their bikes and have their friends over for sleep overs outside in tents, and sharing their fun with their friends....

Their names are K.J. And Braylon and though they were always busy, they were always looking for new things to do...they loved trying new adventures....and their Mother and Father were always happy to see them so close and always enjoying life....She made sure that they cleaned up their room and did other things that were important first and their Father made sure that they did the few chores he had listed for them each day....K.J. And Braylon were wonderful children, loved their parents very much and always did what they were told

One morning, K.J. And Braylon, after eating their breakfast, asked their Mother if it was okay for them to go out into the woods...that they wanted to pretend like they were Daniel Boone and they wanted to go into the woods and see if they could find any deer or squirrels or something exciting....Their Mother laughed and told them it was fine, just to be careful and be home in time for supper....They both grabbed their bow and arrows and ran out the door

They were so excited about being in the woods and seeing some animals and in awe at all the big trees that they had forgot just how far into the woods they had gone, so, they decided it was time to go back home, trouble was, they could not remember which way they had come, they had made so many turns in the woods....They both suddenly realized that they were lost

K.J. Was the the older of the two brothers, so, he held his brother and assured him that everything was going to be okay...After walking for a little while, they decided they would sit down, rest and wait for someone to come and find them...They knew their Mother and Father would be out there looking for them

While sitting under this big tree, they started telling each other stories, told each other about their dreams for when they got bigger and grew up, even their likes and dislikes, sometimes, even with each other, laughed about some friends that they said got on their nerves sometimes, but, really liked them

Well, they talked and talked and talked and suddenly they seen it was getting dark, they had forgotten about the time, and even forgot that they were scared, then they heard people and their names being called, they jumped up yelling and ran into the arms of their loving Mother and Father...They knew they were now safe

That night, they said their prayers, but before they went to sleep, they told each other that this was a day that they would never forget....an experience that had brought them so much closer together

Moral of this story: We all need special time for a one on one

Choosing our words Carefully

We must be careful in the choosing of our word
For once they are spoken, they then have been heard
We cannot then take the words back
By saying, "I am sorry, just give me some slack
Even if spoken in a rage or a moment of outburst
Regardless, they are cruel words that can hurt
Yes cruel words often are quickly spoken
But still, they leave many with a heart that is broken
God gave to us a voice that we could use
But to express ourselves, our emotions, not to abuse
Words can be given for comfort and to give praise
Words of kindness can really make ones day
Give to others words of love that shows your emotion
And the words can also expresses ones devotion
WORDS…choose them wisely, they must be sincere
WORDS…of love and respect are words we all long to hear

Crossing God's Border

Every time we see or hear of a new baby being born
We should all be happy, but why do some of us mourn
Is it because they look at this new life, about to begin
And see them being thrust into a world of greed and sin
Our world has become so insensitive to the need of others
That we no longer consider ourselves, or call
each other, sisters and brothers
Their future and their learnings, should be
taught to them in our schools
But, they are not being taught to learn and to obey the Golden Rule
Instead, they are told who to sing about and to idolize
And to punish or hate the ones whose rules they defy
They are told to sit back, do nothing, only to complain and to whine
For they are being taught to freeload off others,
saying, what is yours, is also mine
They feel they do not have to work, but just sit back
Letting others work harder to take up the slack
Our people need to be taught to stand up and fight
Do not let the Government give them handouts and say, it's alright
We fought for their freedom and their right to speak
For without freedom of choice, we become weak
We need to put God and religion back in our churches and schools
We need to stop letting a minority make us look like fools
Our young people have turned to violence,
robberies, killing whoever they can
Trying to put a scare into, and to intimidate their fellow man
One day, God will say to all those in Government power

Marlene Wheeler Scott

Your day has now come and this is will be your final hour
Jesus said He died and suffered so His people would not
He now needs to let my His people know He has not forgot
So to those of you using your power I say, get your own house in order
For you have defied me, you have now crossed over into My Border

Crystle

You have gone far above and way beyond
Working hard every day, from dusk to dawn
Taking care of not only your own family
But also my very own, just like you took care of me
You have kept your promise to our Mother
That you would take care of us, keeping us always, together
Though sometimes differences caused us to drift apart
We still remained close, always in each others heart
I know that you still feel my presence around
Since God came to move me up to higher ground
Crystle, you now too must move on with your life
Being a good Mother and yes, a good wife
They all need you so very, very much
Wanting you to give them your all, and your loving touch
So, look around you and enjoy your life
Fill it with happiness and love, not with strife
For one day at peace we all will be
When we meet again in Heaven, where forever we now will be

Written for Crystle after her brother Earl passed away,
she was and still is a symbol of strength
In not only her family, but being there to lean on, talk
to and help in all she can for the children
Of Earl..

Marlene Wheeler Scott

Donnie Ray Kennedy
July 20th, 1971—Oct. 17th, 2014

On July 20th, 43years ago upon this earth
To a bouncing baby boy, Faye Kennedy gave birth
She held him close and she said she knew
His life would be special, whatever he chose to do
He met and married Valarie, his lovely wife
Together with family, they both began a new life
They did everything together, were never apart
And he will always be a part of, and remain in her heart
They were looking forward this year, to the 10th of December
It was their special day that they would always remember
For it would have been ten years ago that their new life
Began, as they became, husband and wife
Donnie worked hard for, loved taking care of all his family
His wife Val, son James, LeMont, neice/daughter, Jessica Kennedy
His nieces Erika, Angela, Kayla..nephews..
Kenny, Kevin and Daniel
He was always there for them when needed, he never failed
Donnie's other love was camping in the great outdoors
Riding his four wheeler, fishing and much, much more
And as long as he was surrounded by his family
He was as happy as any man could be
But Donnie's life upon this earth was all too brief
And in it, he had his share of sickness, pain and grief
Sickness and pain became so much a part of his life

God Inspired The Best in Me   43

But, he said he found comfort in his God
and the love of his family and wife
They seen him through so very much
Was always beside him, with support, love and a gentle touch
Donnie grieved so at the loss of Faye, his beloved Mother
But he always knew that one day God would bring them together
Then, the sudden death of Angie, his much loved sister
Not a day went by that he did not mourn and miss her
Today a new life he begins as God calls him away
To reunite with his father Donald, sister Angie,
brother Kenny, his mother, Faye
They will all be waiting for him at Heaven's Door
Saying, "Welcome home Donnie, your
pain and suffering are no more"

**<u>WRITTEN SPECIAL FOR VALARIE KENNEDY,
DONNIE'S WIFE and HIS FAMILY</u>**

Earl

Today we sat quietly as we all said a Prayer
Asking God the question, why, when, and where?
Questions that were asked by each of us
Upon the sudden loss of someone who was loved so much
Today we all stand before God, his family and his friends
Saying good-bye to a loved one whose life so quickly did end
Earl was a loving husband and Father and a devoted brother
Who only wanted peace in his family and
for them to love one another
Yes, Earl would sometimes vent, speak his mind then smile
Saying, "we kept it in the family, that makes it all worthwhile"
When Earl first met Lynette, he knew he would ask her to be his wife
He knew he had found his love, the love of his life
Two beautiful daughters, Raven and Keri, he deeply loved
Thanking God every day for the blessings from above
Corey was his chosen son, he came to love so much
Wanting that special bonding of a Father's touch
Two sisters, Bonita and Crystal, yes, they were very close
He was so proud of them and of them he would often boast
Nieces, nephews, cousins, aunts, uncles, he loved them all
Prayed daily that they would all be ready when Jesus called
A near death experience made Earl realize
that God had given him more time
To be with and near the loved ones he would soon leave behind
Earl had problems, failing health, but, he faced them, he did not run
He said, "I have faith in God, if it be His will, it will be done"
Kenny, his brother-in-law, their closeness could never be denied

Earl knew he had Kenny and God always by his side
Pastor Kenny was always there for him, no matter the time or day
With a warm embrace, to listen, to talk, or just pray
Earl was like a gentle giant, strong but willing to give his all
Loved his God and wanted to be ready when he was called
We know Earl was ready when God called him home
He will always be with us, he never left us alone
As God takes you into the Promised Land
There, your loved ones and your Mother wait
To bring you through Heaven's Gate
Today, we do not say good-bye to Earl, a man we all adored
You will always be remembered until we meet
again, on Heaven's other Shore

WRITTEN FOR THE FAMILY OF
EARL MILES
12/05/12

Faults?

Uh-Oh! You said that I had a fault
OK, I admit it, I guess I got caught
I'm very impatient, this I will admit
Especially with people or things I'd like to forget
I'm also a heavy drinker, this is true
I drink lots of coffee, yes, more than a cup or two
When I get nervous, I bite my nails
And I love going to lots of yard sales
I also tend to stay up pretty late
Taking care of things I could do tomorrow, but can't wait
But, come morning, I do not sleep in
I am up early, cup of coffee, ready for my day to begin
But all in all, I truly believe
That I am me I do not try to deceive
I try to be honest, help anyone, whenever I can
If I see a wrong, I'm not afraid to speak my mind or take a stand
I also believe in God and doing His will
By living for Him and to show everyone that my God is real
Yes, I've lived a long life, and I may be getting old
But, deep down I know that in my Soul
God never found a fault with me
And His is the only opinion that I need
We all have faults, God has forgiven mine
He steps in when I get impatient or out of line
So, if I have offended someone over the years, to you I say
I am sorry forgive me, now, LET US ALL PRAY

Finding Myself

A SLEEPLESS NIGHT, SO MUCH ON MY MIND
MY SANITY, I AM TRYING HARD TO FIND
TAKING ON THE PROBLEMS OF SO MANY
TRYING TO FIND ANSWERS, I
DON'T SEEM TO HAVE ANY

YES, I WANTED TO BE A GOOD
NEIGHBOR AND A FRIEND
SOMEONE ON WHOM PEOPLE COULD DEPEND
I WANTED TO GIVE THEM COMFORT,
A NEEDED WARM EMBRACE
TO HELP THEM THROUGH THINGS,
WE ALL ONE DAY FACE

BUT IN TIME I BECAME TIRED, I
FELT I WAS LOSING TOUCH
ALL BECAUSE I CARED AND I TOOK ON TOO MUCH
I ALWAYS FELT NEEDED, ALWAYS IN DEMAND
I IGNORED ME, AND THINGS JUST GOT OUT OF HAND

Marlene Wheeler Scott

MY FAMILY MY FRIENDS, YOU ALL DID KNOW
THAT I WAS ALWAYS THERE FOR
YOU, ALWAYS READY TO GO
BUT TODAY GOD TOOK MY HAND
AND SAID, I'M STEPPING IN,
YOU NOW NEED TO FIND YOURSELF,
AND TO YOURSELF BE A FRIEND"

I WILL TAKE SOME TIME TO LOOK INSIDE OF ME
FIND THE ANSWERS AND WHAT GOD SAYS WILL BE
WHEN I GET THE ANSWERS AND THE PEACE WITHIN
I WILL THEN BE BACK, I PROMISE YOU MY FRIEND

Finding Time for Jesus

We always seem to find the time for all the things
That it seems like it fills our busy day
But just how much time do we allow
Whenever it comes time to Pray

Jesus just wants what is best for us
He does not want what is leftover, or feel used
For He deserves a place over and above
All the things that we so often choose

So, if we will start each day upon our knees
With only Jesus being on our mind
Then we find peace, our mind will be free
Our rainy days will soon be filled with sunshine

For it is only Jesus that can bring us joy
A joy so unspeakable and so true
But only if we will find time to spend with Him
Can He find the time to spend with me and you

Marlene Wheeler Scott

My First Day of My Summer Vacation

It was the first day of Summer Vacation and Steven wanted to spend the whole day fishing..He had this favorite fishing hole where the fish were always jumping or biting, and sometimes a few others would show up to fish...I wonder if anyone else will be there today? Said Steven as he started out the door...Steven was a very generous young man, he loved to share with others, so, he took an extra fishing pole with him just in case someone needed one

When he got to the fishing hole, no one was there, but, the fish were really jumping, so, Steven sat down, baited his hook and said, "I will just have fun all by myself"

Steven fished all day, caught a lot of fish, but, by now he was getting tired, so, he began to pack up and head for home

That night, as he went to bed, he smiled, remembering how much fun he had this day; and as he knelt and said his Prayers, he said, "Jesus" tomorrow is another day, and what ever I do, I will have fun....and Jesus, thank you for staying with me and helping me to fish....I was learning from the Master.....

Moral:.....When all is said and done
Whether by yourself or alone, you can have fun
Today you had lots of fun, your day you were not wastin'
You enjoyed your first day of your SUMMER VACATION

Frances Elizabeth Williamson
5-17-1949-----8-21-2013

An illness this loving, caring lady fought for so long
Although she struggled, her faith kept her strong
Frankie was a loving Mother, raising her children
in hopes one day she would see
All her children serving God and raising their own family
Frankie did get to see all her children become grown
Seeing each of them getting married, having children of their own
She beamed with pride as she held each and every one
All eleven grand, three great grands, but
still praying for more to come
She held them close to her heart, each in a special place
Thanking God every time she seen their smiling face
Larry, her loving husband, always in her heart and by her side
They had a special bond that could not be denied
Four daughters, Tammy Christine, Cheri and Lynette
All are left now with only memories of a Mother they will never forget
Then, the day came when she heard God say, "I have come for you"
A peace came over her, for she now knew
That God had touched her, taken her by the hand
She was now ready to be taken to the Promised Land
Do not cry for me, I have loved ones who now wait
To welcome me Home as I enter into Heaven's Gate
And I know right in front, waiting with them all
Will be Earl Miles, my very special son-in-law
My final wish is please from God do not ever stray
For I want to see all my loved ones again one day

Marlene Wheeler Scott

Friend to Friend

I called you often, I talked to you
Asking if you needed anything, was there anything I could do
I told you I was someone on whom you could depend
I had a shoulder to cry on, if you needed a friend
One day when I did not call your or stop by
I heard that you sat down and cried
I heard you said I was not there when you were in need
And that you were very upset with me
But, did you ever wonder if I were okay
Or think maybe, I too may have had a bad day
Maybe I needed someone to listen to me
Because, I am not perfect, I have problems too
If you have a friend who really cares
A friend who tries her best, who tries to share
As much of her time that she possibly can
Doing it all willingly, sometimes on demand
Just remember that friendship is a two way street
Somehow, somewhere in the middle, both must meet
For if one day, she should not call or stop by
Then, you go see her, give her a hug, and just say "hi"
Then she too will feel a friendship that has grown
Because friends do not let friends be alone

Friends Forever

My love for you has now passed
We knew it was a love that could not last
For we are of two very different worlds
Who just got caught up in a romantic whirl
You had your ways and I had mine
We could not change or leave the past behind
I truly pray that you will one day meet someone
Enjoying your life together, for life can be fun
Our time together was great while giving us the time to see
Where we were going and what we wanted to be
We both tried to walk that long, long road
But, each step we took, became a heavier load
I now have found and I hope you have too
That special someone, meant for me and for you
Know you will always be special to me, a real good friend
Friends forever, a friendship, I hope will never end

Marlene Wheeler Scott

Friends

Please, do not dream, dreams of me
Because dreams are not what one really sees
You are reaching out to touch someone who is not there
To keep on dreaming and wishing is not fair
For waking up brings to light the reality
That it was only a dream that can never be
I really do not know what else I can do
I have always tried to be honest with you
If I have misled you in any way
I am truly sorry I do not know what else to say
To me a friend is someone in whom you can confide
Dry your tears when you are sad and cry
Someone who will listen to your every word
Making you feel better, knowing you were heard
Someone who comes to your rescue when in need
No questions asked, just saying, "you can count on me"
A friend is unlike a Love that is lost when spurned
A friend asks for nothing in return
Yes, I am a FRIEND, not a dream or a fantasy
And a FRIEND is what I want to be
So, if you are asking about you, my heart and how I feel
I see you only as a very SPECIAL FRIEND who is very real

From Love to Friend

The day that we first met
Is a day that I will never forget
God brings some of us together for a reason
Just like our weather too has a season
Sometimes our love ran hot and then cold
Just like Autumn leaves we too change as we get old
But in between the Winter/Spring and Fall
There is a Summer, lots of love and warmth, that says it all
Then just like seasons, changes we too began to see
That only friends we soon would be
We were bonded by children born out of love
Children God sent to us from above
To be the parents He knew we would be
Yes, He made them to be a part of you and me
In time, our lives changed just like the weather
But, we have a bond that forever will keep us together
Maybe no longer a strong love, this change I regret
But you will always be a friend that I highly respect

Marlene Wheeler Scott

From the Mountain To the Valley to the Mountain

Have you ever found yourself high on the Mountain Top
Admiring all of the riches that you have got?
Then, without warning, you find yourself down in the Valley
Suddenly faced with Truth and Reality
We keep praising God just as long as we got
Whatever it took to get us to the top
But, once we finally made it there
We forget to give thanks to the One who cared
God does not want us to call on Him when just in need
God wants to hear our Prayers, not just our pleas
Everyday we should thank Him for all that to us He is giving
Knowing too, because of Him, we are still living
Only then will you find that your riches will overflow
Then you, on that Mountain Top, again you will go

From This Day Forward

TODAY WAS THE BEGINNING OF A WHOLE NEW LIFE
WHEN BEFORE GOD, WE WERE
PRONOUNCED, HUSBAND AND WIFE
THIS MEANS THAT WE WILL LOVE, HONOR AND OBEY
NOT JUST FOR TODAY, BUT FOR EVERY DAY
TOGETHER OUR HOME WILL BE FILLED
WITH LOVE AND LAUGHTER
BEGINNING NOW AND FOREVER AFTER

CONGRATULATIONS TO THE NEWLYWEDS, MAY YOUR
NEW BEGINNING ALSO BE A BEGINNING WITH GOD
BLESSINGS FROM PASTOR KENNY
&
LAKESIDE OUTREACH MINISTRIES/
KENNETH GRIFFIN MINISTRIES

Getting Older

Sometimes I shrink in fear
Whenever these words I hear
"Grandma", you are really looking your age
You are getting older, like in that final stage
It makes me feel like I am over the hill and done
When I had thought my life again had just begun
I felt I had earned the right to take it slow
After working, raising my children and watching them grow
I felt now I could go on vacation if I wanted to
Doing whatever pleases me, doing what I wanted to do
Well, I may have a wrinkle or two
My hair is turning gray, that certainly is true
My walk, yes, it is a little slower, I do not jog or run
I do not stay up as late as when
I was younger, yes, call it, way back then
But, do not call me old, for I am not
I looked into the mirror and all of me, I still got
When I decide I want to go out on the town
I can still sway to the groove and 'get down'
One thing is true, this you need to hear
God made us wiser, in our Golden year
You may be younger, but there are things you can learn from me
Even if I am in, I admit, my eighties
I am getting older, but, don't you forget
I'm not down yet, on that you can bet

God Is Testing Our Faith

It is true that monies are needed for overhead
But, even in an empty field, your sheep need to be fed
We all need a place to gather praising God in voice and song
It is a place where all who come, get along
God gave us a church, He answered our call
Now we are being tested, to see if we will fall
GOD said we should not close our door, if only for one
Walking through that open day may be the soul that is won
But, the faithful will remain, yes we will
Until again, our church we will again fill
So GOD, we will gather every Sunday to worship and pray
We all have faith, and yes God, we did it Your way

THIS WAS WRITTEN WHEN A DECISION WAS MADE TO OPEN ANOTHER CHURCH WHEN THE ATTENDANCE ON SUNDAYS DROPPED SHARPLY, HOWEVER, OUR PASTOR STILL REMAINS FAITHFUL, OPENING OUR CHURCH DOORS EVERY SUNDAY, EARLY SERVICE TO ALL THOSE WHO STILL COME WHILE STILL PREACHING AT THE NEW CHURCH

Raven 'God's Gift'

I had a Father who, to me was my everything
He protected me from everything that the day would bring
Whether it be happiness or sadness or any fears
He would embrace me, wiping away my tears
Then, suddenly, with the loss of my Father
I felt so alone, wanting to give up, saying, "why bother"?
I became so depressed, I was on a slow decline
Til one day I heard Jesus say, "it is now the time"
The time to send to you someone who
Will change your life, becoming a whole new you"
Then, as God promised, God gave to me a son
Who changed me forever, he became my number '1'
At first I was in complete denial
When I found out that I was indeed with child
I have waited so long for this wonderful day
He would be everything for what I had prayed
The day he was born, I held him so tight
So overwhelmed with both joy and delight
God, I will raise my son right and do the best that I can
My son, I will call him, MY LITTLE, BIG MAN

Raven is the daughter of Earl Miles, GRANDCHILD, LITTLE MAN, BUT, LITTLE MAN WILL BE TOLD ABOUT HIS GRANDFATHER AND ALL THE WONDERFUL MEMORIES HE LEFT BEHIND, IN HIS HEART HE

WILL COME TO KNOW THE GRANDFATHER THAT HE NEVER HAD A CHANCE TO KNOW

Marlene Wheeler Scott

God...Hear My Cry

No one heard me when I cried out
I needed help, I had no doubt
Though I had family, I felt so alone
Please, someone call me on the telephone
I need someone to talk to me
Can anyone hear my cry, my plea?
He said, "I have heard your cry, I am on My way"
He touched my heart and opened my eyes that day
Thank You God, I am getting help at last
When He appeared, things started happening so fast
A new day to me He is now giving
Showing me reasons that I have to go on living
Two beautiful sons, whom I so adore
Friends and family, and yes, so much more
It was I who had lost my way, I was out of control
The old life style I had was taking its' toll
But God, You held on to me, ever so tight
You never let me out of your sight
You made sure I was safe, beside me always, you were near
Though You spoke to me, I did not listen, I did not hear
Then when into that dark hole I began to fall
You showed me, this was my wakeup call
The drugs and partying and all that booze
Was not the life that I had wanted to choose
Now, I am back on solid ground
A new life, thanks to God, I have found
Thank You God for hearing my cry
Upon You, I can always rely and I will never deny

God...I Cried Out to You Today

God, I cried out to you today
Asking you to please, show me the way
I ask you to reach down and touch
All of those whom I love so much
I need to be strong and not be weak
I need to know when I should speak
When they ask me for advise or reach out to me
Asking for my help, whatever it may be
I want to make sure that what I say
Will help them in some way
God, You beside me You would always stand
So, please, as I speak, hold my hand
God, I know that upon You I can always depend
For You are my Protector, my Providor, my Friend
Give me the strength and the words
To speak to my loved ones and let them know they have been heard

Marlene Wheeler Scott

God..I Heard You Speak to Me

God, I cried out to You today and I heard You speak
To me, an immortal who is so weak
You know my weakness and why I keep giving in
Knowing what I am doing is harmful and a sin
It is not because I think this makes me strong
It is just because with the 'in crowd', I wanted to belong
But I still felt so frustrated and so lost
My self values gone, my so called pleasures had it's cost
Then, when I got down, there was no where else to go
I cried out for help, my so called friends became a 'no show'
I dropped to my knees and I began to cry
A voice came to me saying, "why not give God a try"?
So I cried out, "dear God, please,
I want all my sinful ways to cease"
Suddenly there was a struggle, I cannot describe
Surrounding me on every side
But then a warmth came over me, something I had not felt in so long
God had given to me, the strength to be strong
It stayed with me all through the night
Til morning came and I was able to see the light
I looked around, then up to the sky
Saying, "God, I am so glad I found You and gave you a try"
I have now found my rock, my strength, my forever Friend
Someone on whom I know I can always depend
You heard me and You took away my pain and sorrow
I now know with you, I will have a tomorrow

God/Through the Eyes of A Child

God is good and God is kind
God helps us all to stay in line
God sent teachers to set up a Sunday School
God said that we need to obey the Golden Rule
God kicked Adam and Eve out of Garden of Eden when they sinned
God told them to never come back there again
God let David take down a Giant with a sling
And for being obedient, He let him become a King
Then, when Daniel fell into the Lion's Den one day
God showed him how to get out if he just prayed
He healed the sick and made the blind to see
Gave strength to Samson so the slaves he could free
He parted the waters so people could then cross
They wanted their freedom, no matter the cost
God got mad because of sin, said He wanted a new start
So, He showed Noah how to build the Ark
He let it rain for 40 days and 40 nights
God destroyed everything that was left in sight
However, God knew that before things could be complete
He had to do one more thing, His hardest feat
God knew He had to give up His only Son
To suffer for us, if His will was to be done
God is awesome, God is so great
God is always with us when needed, He is never late
Even as a child I know that no matter my need
It will be done if I but let God lead
God, I am so sorry for all your suffering and pain

Marlene Wheeler Scott

But I know if needed you would do it all over again
You say a child sees no wrong, he trusts and believes
That a child is innocent the day they are conceived
God, when I hear or speak Your name, it brings a smile
I thank You God, for letting me be Your child

Happy Birthday T.J.

I met this lady many years ago
And today, I want her to know
That I have really come to respect you
Because of the many things that you do
Your Faith in God cannot be denied
In all your trials, He has stayed by your side
Our friendship, yes it grew and grew
Because I seen you as one of a few
Who never said no to anyone, you always had time
And if needed, you would give them your last dime
Your words of wisdom I really have nourished
I have felt blessed, as our friendship has flourished
So, today I want to take time
To say something special to this friend of mine
God Bless you on this, your very special day
!!!!HAPPY BIRTHDAY!!!!..my forever friend, T.J.

I met T.J on Polly's Landing about fourteen years ago...She was the owner and she gave our Pastor a building to start Sunday Worship on the Lake and this became the beginning of our church, known as
LAKESIDE OUTREACH MINISTRIES

Marlene Wheeler Scott

Hello Bubba

Hello Bubba, I heard you calling my name
It sounds like you are trying to find someone to blame
Bubba, everything you have said I know is true
And I am taking the time God has given me to talk to you
Yes, God put us together, though it was not for long
But in our time together, we had a bond between us that was strong
We talked, played games, did many things together
We were really good for each other
Then one day, suddenly, God called me home
But Bubba, when I left, I did not leave you alone
You have brothers and sisters who like to argue and fuss too
But, no matter what, they will always be there for you
Your Mother, she needs you, she could use a helping hand
From you Bubba, her son, her strong little man
Your Grandmother, she really loves you so
I feel that it is to her home for a while you will go
Brighter days I see are ahead for you
You just need to take it slow, do not rush it through
God chose us to be together for a reason
And we will weather this together, no matter the season
Come Winter, Summer, Spring or Fall
Remember, you are in this world for the long haul
Bubba, you have so much to others that you can give
But first, you must tell yourself, I am alive and I want to live

You are still my Homeboy, and you know what that means
We do not come unraveled at the seams
We hang in there when the going gets rough
Because we believe, we are Homeboys and we are tough

BUBBA, I AM NOW TURNING OFF THE
LIGHT….GOOD NIGHT…LOVE YOU
EVERYTHING IS GOING TO BE ALRIGHT

Marlene Wheeler Scott

Hello Mother

I know that I can never ease your pain
I know will now never be the same
Mother, so many things I could not talk about
I was becoming fearful, I was having so many doubts
There seemed to be so much confusion,
my life was going out of control
I felt myself weakening, as things began to unfold
Mother, I was beginning to feel so much strife
With all these changes, beginning to happen in my life
God says that it is He who knows the time that we must go
I felt this was the day, but, before I left, I wanted you to know
I did not leave before I said 'good-bye'
To you Mother, who loved me and who really tried
I also said 'good-bye' to Cody, my only brother
Asking you both for forgiveness, and for him
to take care of you, our Mother
Then, to God, to Him all my sins I confessed
I wanted my Soul to be free and at rest
Mother, I see you sharing your pain with so many others
Talking to groups, trying to bring other families together
This is my first Mother's Day that from you I will be away
But, I know I am in your heart, where I will forever stay
I also know Mother that today you will also share
Your pain, your sorrow, your love with all Mother's everywhere
Who has lost a child before their time
Leaving so many precious memories of them behind
Mother, I know that it is in the Spirit I come today

Knowing that you will know I am with you as I say
You were the Best Mother a son could ever had
I do not want this special day of yours to be sad
This day you will share with Cody, your wonderful son
Know we both love you, you will forever be 'number one'
HAPPY MOTHER'S DAY

WRITTEN FOR DANE AND CODY'S MOTHER...DANE TOOK HIS LIFE THE DAY AFTER MOTHER'S DAY IN 2014.... WORDS I FELT HE WANTED TO SAY TO HIS MOTHER, THIS FIRST MOTHER'S DAY IN 2015 WITHOUT HIM

Hello To All My Family
Earl

To my family and friends I want to say
I may be gone, but, I am not that far away
The reunion I had here when I arrived
Is one to be shared, cannot be described
One day there will be a gathering for us all
When God blows His trumpet saying, "last call"
I know I still live within your heart
And because of that, we will never be apart
I love my family that I left behind
But, I know I will see you all again, in God's time
A grandson I now have, my first one
Already, this old heart he has won
I know you all will celebrate my memory today
With a cookout, now, that is the way
When you celebrate, and I know you will
Cause I can see Crystal getting out the grill
Telling everyone to come over for this special cookout
With Earl's memory, with his family, that is what it is all about
Yes, family and friends, grilling, eating, what more can I say
Except, I wish this could be done every day
To my two girls, Raven and Keri I want to say
I thanked God for each of you, every day
For the time He let me spend with you
Until God called me home, but said He would see you through
Raven, you have truly me me so proud
I heard the Heaven's ring out and the clapping of thunder so loud

The day you gave birth to my first grandson
A Blessing to you too, your first, forever would be your number one
Keri, God said that He wants you to know
He has given to you a heart that continues to grow
Though to yourself, your worthiness you seem to deny
Your hurt and your true feelings, you try to hide
You love people, especially children, your nieces and nephews
They love you and they have come to depend upon you
One day, unexpected, you are going to find
Your dream come true, it will be one of a kind
My little 'Redhead', so quiet and shy
Whenever asked for help, would smile and say, "I'll try"
So, Keri, do not give up, keep your head held high
Smile, give your 'ole' Daddy a hands up, a 'Hi-Fi'

Corey, troubles too, in your young life you have embraced
But, together we met them, face to face
A wonderful son you were to me
Just let your past go, it is now just history
You just need to know that God is near
And when you pray, your prayer God will hear
To me, the best thing that ever happened to me
Was God giving to me a family
For who I would gladly have given my life
For my children and my wife
Life is short for all of us
PLEASE, remember you are a family, keep in touch

Earl Miles

I Always Have Time

My friend, I always have time for you
No matter what you need me to do
When you are in need, you just need to reach out
Just give me a call, or just give me a shout
If you are ever sick and you need someone
Just call on me, you know that I will come
My schedule I can always adjust to find the time
To help out a friend of mine
You are a friend and you know I care
So, if you need me, just call and I will be there
God said an appointed time He has for us all
When we are needed, upon us He will call

I call my book, Devotion/Words in Motion for many
reasons..These words/set in poem are written about
everything from birth, to death, marriage, anniversaries,
religion, personal, Ordinations, and yes, even political
They were written for friends, family, loved ones, and
many at the request of strangers…Many said they found
consolation, peace, and comfort in these poems.. I thank God
for giving me these words…I promised God my Devotion
and He gave me the words to write, to Put into Motion
I feel that God has given to me a "Gift", if you will, to be able to
express in words, the pain/happiness/ and sadness of others, even
to giving words to them from a loved one who has passed on
I have even been given words of things regarding freedom of speech
or the right to worship in our own way, about Prayer and War
Yes, someone once said that <u>The Pen is Mightier than the
Sword,</u> and I truly believe that to be very true, especially
when God is guiding every stroke of the pen, so, I pray that
you can identify with, or find comfort in any of these poems
that I have written with much Love and Devotion
I give to you my last book
DEVOTION/WORDS IN MOTION
A SPIRITUAL AWAKENING

I Cried out to my Jesus

JESUS, JESUS, I cried out your name
Crying, please tell me, am I to blame
Was it my sins that caused the loss
Of your life when they nailed to the Cross?
So many tears I have cried whenever I see
Just how much you suffered for me
Please God, show me now what I can do
To become more worthy of you
I now know the suffering you did for me
Was so that one day I too would be free
Yes dear Jesus, my life to you I now want to give
So one day in Heaven, with you forever, I will live

I'm Sorry

TO MY LOVED ONES, I SEE SO MUCH
PAIN AND HEARTACHE
I KEEP ASKING MYSELF, "WHAT WILL IT TAKE"?
TO EASE THIS BITTERNESS AND WIPE AWAY THE TEARS
FOR I DO NOT WANT THESE PAINFUL
DAYS TO TURN INTO YEARS
I KNOW I DID SO MANY THINGS WRONG
I ADMIT, I WAS WEAK, I WAS NOT STRONG
I SHOULD HAVE TRIED HARDER DURING MY LIFE
TO HAVE BEEN A BETTER MOTHER,
A MORE LOVING WIFE
WITH ALL MY HEART, I ASK FOR YOUR
FORGIVENESS AND YOU TO KNOW
THAT I DID, AND I DO, STILL LOVE YOU ALL SO
MY HUSBAND EARL, WHO LOVED ME
UNCONDITIONALLY, I REGRET
I CANNOT ASK FOR YOUR FORGIVENESS,
BUT YOUR LOVE I'LL NEVER FORGET
TO MY FRIENDS AND FAMILY WHO HAVE STOOD BY ME
"THANK YOU", I AM TRYING TO CHANGE, YOU WILL SEE
TO MY CHILDREN, COREY, RAVEN,
KERI, I KNOW THAT I NOW MUST
AGAIN EARN YOUR LOVE AND YOUR TRUST
I KNOW THAT IT WILL NOT BE EASY
FOR ALL OF YOU TO AGAIN BELIEVE AND TRUST IN ME

BUT PLEASE, WORK WITH ME AND THIS
BATTLE WE WILL OVERCOME
AND WITH GOD'S HELP, WE WILL BE
A FAMILY, UNITED AS ONE
SO PLEASE, WE ARE A FAMILY AND
WE NEED EACH OTHER
EARL LOVED US ALL AND HE WOULD
WANT TO SEE US TOGETHER

<u>WRITTEN FOR LYNETTE MILES</u>
<u>APRIL 02, 2013</u>

It's Time We Have Our Say

I have something that I want to say
About today, the start of a brand new day
Will it be about politics, scandals, or even me
Or about the war in some other country
It is so hard to obey the Golden Rule
Since our Government took Prayer out of our school
Our corporate scandals are getting so bad
They are taking away what monies the average American had
Even our elected officials turn the other way
When their own is found to be taking bribery and pay
We sponsor a war that many say is unjust
Costing lives and money, some call it Iran or Bust
They have no worry that it is costing us every penny
Those in the know are getting fat, the taxpayers are getting skinny
Our supreme courts are elected to be fair to us all
To speak for the majority, thereby enforcing our law
But, no, they chose to rule for the favor of some
So, where is the Justice, called, "one for all, all for one"
America need to get back on track
By putting Religion, Trust and Honor back
Back into our schools, elected offices and all that lack
The integrity and backbone, or having the spine
To stand up for what is right and not to whine
America means justice and being free
For every Americans, not just for me
Also, if you break our laws, then you must pay

Marlene Wheeler Scott

For that is the American way
How about those immigrants crossing out border
And causing within our land, so much disorder
They take away the things that are ours
Like jobs and aide by using our justice power
To me the answer is very easy
As easy as saying, one-two-three
If you come here and you know you do not belong
You are breaking our laws, you know you are wrong
So, back you will go when you are found
We ask that our elected officials do not let us down
Because they get so busy, they want to appease
The countries you come from but are against us, you see
But, who do they call upon when they are in need
Good old America, the land of the free
We need to get back to being strong
And put US back in power where we belong
Freedom is ours, it is our choice
And with freedom, we have a voice
Our laws should be for the majority
Not for one or two or a minority
So let our voices all ring out
Stand up for freedom and to our leaders shout
We have elected you, so it is us you should defend
But, if you cannot, then the power we gave you must end

Keri/Raven/Corey

To my children, I have watched the year play out
I still see you all in mourning, so much in doubt
I wanted the best for all of you
I only wish there was more I could do
But, staying in mourning will not help
Do not rely on others you must do for your self
You are a part of me, my generation to carry on
My two daughters and my son
A grandchild has now been added to our family
Making us now, generation number, three
So, I ask you all to please take care of each other
Live your life for God, so one day, we will all again be together

Written for Ker1, Raven, Corey upon the
one year remembrance of their
Father, Earl Miles who passed away/ Dec. 2012

Marlene Wheeler Scott

Kyla

As I hold your hand and look at you today
Please know it is from my heart, these words to you, I say
God brought us together, and for fourteen years
We have found much happiness, and weathered many tears
But, as our years together keeps getting longer and longer
Our love for each other, also just gets stronger and stronger
The day we first met, you became the APPLE of MY EYE
For you stirred within me, a love I could not deny
Without you Kyla, I am nothing, being
with you makes me feel whole
That is why I love you Kyla, with all my heart and soul
Today, before family, friends and the good Lord above
I vow again to you, my eternal love

Lest We Forget

Someone is forgetting that this is a country of choice
And everyone in it has a voice
But suddenly, we are being told what to wear
If we get sick, we have to have Obama Care
Well if we get sick, surely we would all know
Who our Dr. is and where we should go
We have welcomed here everyone, from all around
Even the Illegals who have come on America's ground
We elected officials who were to take care of us
But, somehow when they got to Washington, they lost touch
We are now being told in what or who to believe
They are letting them take away our place to worship or grieve
Banning our Christmas Holidays and caroling, an American tradition
Closing our shelters and even our missions
Saluting our Flag has become a NO-NO
Respect for our Veterans has hit a new low
Now they are choosing the foods that we eat
No more chocolates, candy, cookies or anything sweet
Taking away foods we want, they say it is making us fat
Now what kind of government is that?
If we want something, we need permission, now let me understand
We do not know what is good for us, so,
Big Brother has to hold our hand
Well, I am not a child and my body belongs to me
I do not want Big Brother, my Government telling me what I need
If I no longer can eat, think, live my life, then, I am no longer free

Marlene Wheeler Scott

I might as well be dead, but, it was not the
sweets and fats that killed me
And the cruelty of mankind has reached its peak
There can be no more peace and then, only death will we seek
So, when I die, do an autopsy on me
And the cause was will be found to be
Due to lack of freedom, the heart gave up, it finally ceased
For only in death, would I find peace and be me

Letting God In

This morning I awoke with great anticipation
I was waiting to get out of my bed
I was no longer afraid of what temptation
I would find before me on the road ahead

Somehow I just knew that on the darkest day
The Sun would surely, brightly shine
I knew I only needed to let God lead the way
For I trusted Him and He was more than a friend of mine

God never left me He was always by my side
He always found a way to fill my empty heart
And this day I knew my prayer to Him would not be denied
As I cried out to Him, "oh God, how great Thou art"

Today God sent me down this path
That would change the rest of my life
God sent a friend that would again make me laugh
Help me as I struggled through my pain and strife

God, I give thanks and praise to You every day
For all your love and for filling my empty heart
I now know if we do not let God in or open that door
Then we will never find the peace and love that we are searching for

Marlene Wheeler Scott

Looking for the Door

Did you ever keep trying to open a door
Hoping on the other side, you find what you are looking for?
But, once it was opened, to your surprise
You discovered it had always been there before your very eyes
It is just that sometimes we take things for granted
Letting our views of things to sometimes become slanted
Judgement calls on others then we tend to make
Forgetting that we too have made mistakes
We are never satisfied we keep wanting more and more
We keep trying to find what is behind that other door
Once we find that door and we go inside
We find those things that to us have never been denied
God said that your heart is that door
That had to be opened before you find what you are looking for
God said that the key to open that door
Was a forgiving heart, that you are looking for
Forgiveness must come from the heart, from within
Without forgiveness, God says in Heaven you cannot enter in

God Inspired The Best in Me

Love Cannot Be One Way

If I give to you my love and tell you that I care
It will be a love that only you and I should share
My love is not based on what I can get
But of lasting memories I never want to forget
I prayed that I would find someone like you
God answered my prayer and today we said "I do"
It is a commitment we have made to each other
Not to be broken and shared by a friend, a sister or a brother
For me, I can only love one at a time
And I will love you as long as you are only mine
There will be no forgiveness if I ever lose your trust
Or accepting your excuse, it was not love it was only lust
For when you let the flesh become a form of desire
Then it tends to make you a cheat and a liar
Adam and Eve were happy til the Serpent crawled in
Convincing them the naked body was a
temptation for some to stray
But God never wanted our bodies used in that way
God never wanted the flesh to be used
for temptation and pleasure
But for the bonding of love and creating new life
Joining together as one, husband and wife

Marlene Wheeler Scott

Love Is

Love is a word that is so freely used
Love is a word that we sometimes abuse
Love is so freely spoken, thrown around
Love is a word that can make you feel good or let you down
Love, in so many languages it is spoken
Love can create a marriage, or cause one to be broken
Love should be sincere when shown or given to a friend
Love should be unconditional, it should never end
Love means different things to all of us
Love means affection, friendship, and trust
Love can sometimes seem like it is controlling
Love can make some feel like they have to be, beholding
Love is a word we all long to hear
Love should come from the heart, it must be sincere

Misunderstood
Choosing my Words

Why do people say, "I'm not sure of what I just said
Whatever it was, I think into the words, people just misread"
Yes, I was angry and the words that I wrote
Certainly did not get me a popularity vote
So to those who knew the words were meant just for you
I say I am sorry for posting it for all to view
It is all over and done and if I ever do it again
I promise to call you first before I post and send
So to all the others who would take this route
Be careful what you say, let your words leave no doubt
Sometimes words that are supposed to be a compliment
Can be misunderstood, not what you meant
Choose them wisely, think them through
You will get more respect from others when you do

My Child

Lynette, I see your heart, you are feeling so alone
You feel lost, there is no place you can call home
My child, I heard your prayers and I heard your cry
But you must believe, it is who you must try
For I have sent down Angels as you asked me too
But you pushed them aside, wanting them to stay away from you
The Devil has put you in His chains
Hoping to bring you down into His hell of flames
Now, only you can take control
Over who is going to take your soul
You can stand up straight, hold your head up high
Tell Satan leave me, for my Savior I will no longer deny
Yes, he will hang around just to make sure
But will leave quickly when he sees your heart is again pure
I am here with you always, you will never be alone
And one day you can call Heaven your home

My Classmates Of "55"

When I look back at this memorable year in time
So many of my classmates that year come to mind
Though some of them have gone on and it saddened us
They too are remembered, they are missed so very much
Our reunions are fantastic, when so many of us gather here
To go over and catch up on memories we hold so dear
To all the young men who were in my class
I think of all of you as, a "first class act"
To the young ladies of my class, just a word or two
I thank you for just being you
Barbara, Alice, Donna, Diane
Dixie, Gertrude, Hazel, Mary Anne
Betty, Inez, and not forgetting Alice number #2
Words cannot express how much I appreciate all of you
Not only were we classmates, but we were
friends who bonded together
And through the years we managed to
stay in touch with each other
Though I do not get to see you all very much
We still write or call, but somehow, we keep in touch
God gave me words, I wrote some of them for you
About your loved ones passing, which were my classmates too
You all soon became a part and a reason for this book of mine
I will never forget you, you all will always
be in my heart and on my mind

Marlene Wheeler Scott

My Friend..Polly McLeod

My heart skipped that day when
I first met Polly, who would forever become my friend
My feelings and fears with her I soon shared
Because I knew she really cared
She was an unexpected friend, who yes indeed
Reached out to me in my time of need
She took me in also as part of her family
Saying, "God says we are like sisters, you and me"
But Polly is not only a friend to just me
She is always there for anyone in need
She will visit them in the hospital, or in their home
Bringing the word of God, assuring them they are not alone
I wish that we could see each other much more
Be nice if we lived close, like maybe next door
But we still call, keeping in touch
I enjoy this time with a friend that I have come to love so much
Polly, I want you to know that you are the reason
I began enjoying life, no longer thinking of leaving
God, I know sometimes when I pray
I fail to say thank you for sending Ms. Polly my way
So, before God and all I want to say I am so proud
To be a part of her life and have a friend like Polly Mcleod

I TRULY BELIEVE THAT GOD SENDS PEOPLE INTO
OUR LIVES WHEN WE NEED SOMEONE
AND GOD BROUGHT POLLY INTO MY LIFE THROUGH
ANOTHER FRIEND, HER SISTER-IN-LAW
SHIRLEY McLEOD WHO HAS GONE ON TO BE
WITH HER HEAVENLY FATHER

God Inspired The Best in Me

My Mother

She was a beautiful lady, with a lovely smile
She was there for us, always walking that extra mile
She always listened to our concerns and little whines
But reminded us that some things could only be learned in time
She told us to always try and do our very best
To put our trust in God and He would do the rest
For in this world in which we now live
We must learn to let go, forget and forgive
Her teachings and her love she gave to us all
To both family and friend, if needed,
she said, "just give me a call"
Though she has gone, yes, but not even death
Could take away the teachings and memories that she has left
I still feel her presence, her warmth and loving touch
She was my Mother that I loved so very much

WRITTEN FOR LISA ON THE ANNIVERSARY
OF HER MOTHER'S DEATH
GOD BLESS

Marlene Wheeler Scott

Patti

You say that you are depressed, that you are feeling blue
Well, let me tell you, what you should do
Go outside and look to the Heaven's high
Ask God your question, "God Why"?
Your heart will then begin to race
You will feel a smile come across your face
Somehow I think that you already knew
But you just wanted to feel it when God gave the answer to you
God touched your face, the smile the answer in God you did find
That after every storm, God always sends the Sunshine
Many storms through your life have passed
But, God also sent you Sunshine, the storms did not last
With the Sunshine came many Blessing given to you
A family whose love brought you through
So, when it is answers to questions you need to find
Remember, God will be there, He knows what is on your mind
So wake up in the morning with a smile on your face
Saying, "whatever is ahead today, I will embrace"
The birds are singing and telling me all is well
With God beside me, I cannot fail
So, good morning world, it is for you I will pray
That you too have a Blessed and Peaceful day

Polly McLeod

Eighty four years ago, into this world
Was born, a bouncing, healthy, baby girl
God already had plans laid out for her
She was His chosen that was for sure
Throughout her life, she did as God had deemed
In return, God blessed her and fulfilled her dreams
She married a young man that she loved
Their reunion became one that was made in Heaven above
Many children, in birth to her were given
Made their lives even more worth livin'
Eight children total, three girls and five boys
Filled their lives with so much happiness and joy
They were so proud of all of them
She raised them all to know God and to have faith in Him
She has had her share of health problems, this is true
But, she knew that her God would always see her through
She continued to pray and to help others
Considered all God's children, her sisters and brothers
So many lives over the years she has touched
This woman of God who is loved so very much
I am one of those whose life she touched and I am so proud
To call her my sister in Christ, my friend, POLLY McLEOD
!!!!!!!!!!!HAPPY BIRTHDAY!!!!!!!!!!!!!
84…God Bless you with many more

Rainy Day Friends

I think it is cruel and not really fair
To tell someone you love them and that you care
But, when you are needed, you're never around
It seems like you just do not want to be found
I need a friend in whom I can confide
When I am going through a storm, they don't run and hide
For a friend is someone upon whom you depend
When you ask them for help, they readily say, "where and when?"
Rainy day friends will also one day need
A true friend, yes, they may even remember me
But, if I am your friend, and I tell you so
I do it from the heart, not just for show
So, if you tell a friend, you love them and you care
Tell them also, "if you need me, I will be there"

Raising Our Flag and Our Voices

Let us raise our Red-White-and Blue
Against all of those who are trying to
Take away our freedom in this, our own land
We need to lift our voices and take a stand
For over 200 years, many have died and fought
For freedom of Religion and schools where
our children would be taught
We cried out, this is our land, we all have freedom here
We can Pray, teach, and vote, making our voices heard without fear
There are many with dreams who are still coming from afar
Saying only in America, can we reach for the stars
We can worship freely, be whatever we choose to be
Sending our children to college, raising a family
Sadly, we are still fighting for things here have gone too far
Many of our voices, some in our Government has tried to bar
The laws are neglecting the majority, favoring a very few
More and more Americans are crying out, "what can we do?'
We can come together, raising our flag again and using our voice
To let our Government know, we elected you, we do have a choice
The perks and monies that you get to appease a few
Will soon be over, yes, our voices being quieted is long overdo
Because we will stand together, whether we
are here by birth or by choice
For this is our country, and freedom means that we all have a voice

Marlene Wheeler Scott

Rev. Leo Tidwell
1933-2014

I wanted to write a word or two
I wanted to find the right words to choose
For here was a man who was very respected
Because from his God and his Faith, he never defected
When God called upon him to spread his word
He went to the airwaves so he could really be heard
God blessed him with a family that he loved so
He would smile and thank God as he watched his family grow
24 Grand, 28 Great Grands and 01 Great-Great Grand
Leo said they were his future, all part of God's plan
God called him home, but now you will see
His legacy and the Tidwell Ministry
His beloved family will continue to carry on
All the work that Rev. Tidwell had begun
We know that you have now gone to Heaven to make a place
For all of us, where we will again meet each other face to face
Today you heard the Angels ringing that Golden Bell
Saying "welcome home" REV. LEO TIDWELL

WRITTEN FOR THE CHILDREN AND ALL THE
FAMILIES OF REV. LEO TIDWELL
GOD'S BLESSINGS AND COMFORTS TO EACH OF YOU AT THIS TIME
<u>REST IN PEACE</u>
<u>YOUR MEMORIES AND WORK WILL NEVER CEASE</u>

God Inspired The Best in Me

Robert

Robert, my heart melted the day we first met
It is a day, I will never forget
You reminded me of a sweet, cuddly TEDDY BEAR
I just wanted to squeeze you and tell you how much I cared
And when you held me, you made me feel
Like a woman, and I knew your love for each other was real
Today, fourteen years later, our vows we renew
In front of God, family, friends, sharing my love for you
Our children bonded our love, our shelter became a home
A bond that said we're together, we will never be alone
So, here today, before God and man I again say
I love you Robert, forever, today and everyday
As I place my hand in your hand again
I share your love, taking us to heights, we have never been
I LOVE YOU

Robert

Fourteen years ago when we first met
It became the beginning of my life, a day I will never forget
I fell in love with you then, I love you still
I always have and I always will
You gave to me a home, a family, someone to love
I know it was all because of a blessing from above
I call you my special TEDDY BEAR, this is true
Because they are so loveable and huggable, and so are you
Friends and family are to share with us today
As we stand before God, and again we get to say
Our vows of love to one another
To always be faithful and true to each other
So, as I place my hand in your hand again
Our love is renewed today, to heights we have never been
I love you Robert Watford
My wonderful, lovable
TEDDY BEAR

My Time With God

I set aside a special time every day
To talk to my God and to pray
I would not allow anything to interfere
When my Praying time would come near
I would watch the clock, waiting for the time
When I would talk to God, telling Him what was on my mind
I would then hear a quiet voice say to me, "you know that I care
I too am waiting to hear your Prayer"
But after He listened to my Prayer today
He said "you now must listen to what I have to say"
"Why do you sit aside a special time each day with Me
When you know I am with you always, no matter your need"
Yes, I want you to have that special, quiet time
To spend with me and get peace of mind
But, the time you set aside should not always be
The only time you choose to talk to me
Prayer should be genuine and from the heart
From this, I never want you to part
You can call on me any time, just say, "God, I need you now"
Do not feel that you have to wait until your chosen time rolls around

Marlene Wheeler Scott

The Day In The Life Of A Mother

I have so many errands today to run
I am already tired, but, I have just begun
I must taxi my children off to school
Pick up some of their friends they said "a few"
Grocery shopping that is next on my list
Checking it twice, making sure there is nothing I missed
Then back home to do the laundry, clean and dust
That is on my list too, and that is a must
Okay, I'm done with that and just in time
Off to school to pick up the children, I hope just mine
They said that they had plans, not to be late
Because they did not have time to stand around and wait
Well, here I am back home
The children are gone, I am again alone
They said, "be back in time for supper, make it a surprise"
Works for me, I will just fix hamburgers and fries
The day is over, everyone has now settled in
I am now going to relax, soak in the tub and then
Rest and get ready for tomorrow, another day
And if anyone asks me why, I will simply say
Every day I am with, and can do for my family I discover
This is not work, I really love, being a Mother

To All My Brothers And Sisters
JUNE 11TH, 2013

Being asked to write a letter to our Mother, and for Mother's Day, to write about our memories of her I truly did not understand..I do understand about gathering together, or get togethers where we would all remember and talk about Mother and share memories, happy and sad, cry and laugh with each other, sharing childhood memories, we all have really different ones, the first five of us would have total different memories than the last five children, but, memories of Mother all the same, very much loved

We all loved our Mother very much and were Blessed to have her with us for so long, to see her and to do things with her, some more so than others, but we were all proud of our Mother

I speak/talk to Mother every single day and there is not enough words or paper to be able to write about Mother..what I think would be nice is that each brother and sister start writing a journal about your memories of Mother and then passing it on to each of your children and grandchildren, therefore letting them to be able to tell stories of and about their Grandmother Stella, all generations love hearing these stories of grandparents and great grandparents, etc..it keeps the memories alive

However, if you are wanting me to write something down on paper to tell you how I feel or felt about Mother, no problem...three little words...I loved her and I miss her... it comes from the heart, not just words on paper to be read

Marlene Wheeler Scott

I do not know as of this writing if I will be there with you when you gather in Kentucky in Sept...I do not and cannot make plans that far in advance...I am in hopes of being there with you...I know you all will have a great time and and a wonderful family gathering love...I do love you all

I close this letter with much prayer, lots
of love and God's Blessings
Your sister/////////////Marlene

To All My Family

I know that it has been almost a year
Since I left earth and those that I loved so dear
But, here, there is no such thing as time
While on earth, it is always on our mind
We do not know the time or even when
Our time on earth, will suddenly end
So it was that eventful day with me
When I unexpectedly left home and all of my family
I see your pain, your hurt, and so much crying
I see some of you giving up hope, not even trying
Trying to accept what happened, why I am no longer there
Even blaming God, saying that He did not care
God is a caring God who has let you take a quick glance
At your lives, and is giving you a second chance
He says you must love one another, do all that you can
Even saying, I forgive you and I do understand
You must stay right with God, living your life
Free of hatred, doubts and so much strife
It is only then that when all of this has ceased
That you will find God and an inner peace
Do not cry for me, for I am in a better place
No longer a part of the Human Race
I have met some of my friends, and my family
My Father Q.L., cousin Earl, and even Uncle J.C.

Marlene Wheeler Scott

We are all looking forward to the day when
We will be reunited and together once again
And when those Pearly Gates begin to open wide
We'll be waiting, saying Welcome, please come inside

**Written to the family and loved ones of Kevin Evans
After his sudden passing**

Uncle Joseph

Uncle Joseph, I keep calling your name
Nothing here seems to be the same
It has been a long time since here you stayed
Can you come back so that we can again play?
I remember I got up one morning, you were not there
I looked for you, everywhere
Then people started gathering around
All I could hear were crying sounds
I heard someone say, Joseph is gone
We do not know yet what is wrong
I was young and I became so confused
All I remember is that I started crying too
I began to sit alone in my room at night
You were not there to turn off the light
For I did not have you there to say
Bubba, turn off the light, sleep well, it's okay, tomorrow is another day
I just need you to please come and talk to me
I want once again to be with someone I can believe
I feel like I am becoming a real mess
I have so much I want to get off my chest
I know it is upsetting my Mom and Grandma
I also know they want what is good for me, that is all
But, you and I were Homeboys, we could communicate
We loved to talk and also to debate
So, Uncle Joseph, I will sit in my lighted room again tonight

Waiting for you to come, turn off the light, saying, it will be alright
Assuring me that yes, tomorrow is a new day
And I can handle anything that comes my way
I not only want you to be proud of me
But also my Grandmother, Mother and all my family
This I promise to all of you, I will try
As long as I know you are all here, by my side

Who is She?

She keeps busy in lots of ways
Sometimes, even wishing she had more days
She works so hard, she is always in so much demand
That she asks God to help her out as much as He can
She is active in all our Church deeds
Helping us to plant and sow God's seeds
Seeds that will help our Church to really grow
And she does it for God, not for show
She has put us all together, no, not in print
Can you name her?, here, I will give you a hint
She took a string of yarn, made a blanket of love
Working for hours with God's guidance from above
When she was finished God smiled, saying "well done"
Mother of my Shepherd, my appointed one
In this blanket you have joined us all as one
Mother, Father, sister, brother, daughter and son

++++THE SHEEP AND THE BLANKET BOTH HAVE A FOLD
AND BOTH CAN BE UNRAVELED IF ONE IS NOT TOLD
THAT IF THE BLANKET BEGINS TO FRAY
OR THE SHEEP BEGIN TO STRAY
THEN THE KNITTER MUST KNIT AND
THE SHEPHERD MUST PRAY++++

Marlene Wheeler Scott

A Witch's World

Tressa was a 14 year old girl who met three witches by lighting a black flame candle...their names were Ashley, Britany, and Tori

The witches took Tressa back to their home, in HalloweenVille, USA...It was Halloween night there and this was the night where anything could come back to life

They knew all the Demons and Warlocks would come back, but, because they had vanquished them before, they felt certain they could do it again...However, there was one Demon they were worried about because he was not dead, but very much alive, his name was Royce while he was on this earth, but, when he was with his own kind, he became known as Steven and he became invisible...He was invisible because he used to be the source of all evil..though two demons had offered him new powers where he would be invisible forever he refused, but the demons gave him the power anyway

The Witches became so worried about him that they tried to go back to the real world by opening the portal, but, Steven closed the portal on them, so now, they knew they were stuck in Halloween Ville

Steven even tried to kill Tressa by throwing a fireball at her, but, she blocked it by using her powers, powers that she did not even know she had, then Tressa turned and ran back to the house where Ashley, Britany and Tori all lived

They then took out the book of shadows to study and to see if there was a poison or something that they could fix to kill Steven, forever this time, but, Steven had followed them to their house and screamed out, "you witches will never defeat Steven"

Tressa knew they would never get away from Steven until he was dead

Tori was finally done with one of the poisons and when she lifted the roof of the house, blue smoke poured out due to the poisons, but nothing happened, so, she threw it all out, still nothing happened... Tori said, "maybe if we combine all the poisons I have made to kill all evil with the one I just made, it may be powerful enough to kill him, and Britany yelled, "yes, it just might work".....About that time, Tressa yelled out, "oh no" and Ashley asked her, "what is it?" and Tressa said, "there is a tree coming toward us and is going to kill us with it's branches", and as the tree came closer, Tressa turned her head just as it was about to chop off her head... "Hey, leave her alone" yelled Tori, who then yelled to Ashley to look after and take care of Tressa...Ashley then turned and killed the tree.... "Tori, hurry up with the poisons, we cannot hold Steven off much longer Finally, Tori was done and they began throwing the poisons at Steven, but Steven had possessed the pumpkin and used it to block the poisons causing them to spill all of it

So now, they all knew they would have to stand and fight, so, they all positioned themselves for the fight...Tori elevated herself up and kicked Steven, Britany then froze him and Ashley moved him somewhere else, but nothing was working, so Tressa, having found she had powers also, but not knowing how powerful they were, decided to use them....Tressa was able to Orbit, so, she held onto Steven and orbited him back to the past....Then, Ashley, Britany, and Tori wrote a spell that would send them back into time also ....Once there, they found Tressa and told her they had brought the poisons with them and together, they went to find Steven...When they found him, they all threw the poisons on him and he died....they were now free and they could go back home and the future, which they all did

Ashley, Britany, and Tori then all waited for the Sun to rise the next morning and when it did and nothing happened, they knew it meant they could now go back and Tori laughed and said to the others, I will see you all again next Halloween Then, Tressa awoke, but, she was thinking that it had all been a dream until she seen a note by her bedside that said "thanks for the adventure and we will see you again next year.... We had a B-Witching good time....Ashley...Britany....Tori

You

YOU have given me extra strength, YOU have given me love
YOU have given me many blessings from above
YOU have held me when I have cried out
You have answered my questions when I was in doubt
YOU never left me, YOU kept holding my hand
YOU gave me comfort, I knew YOU would understand
YOU kept reaching down to embrace me
YOU said YOU would stay with me and never leave
Who is this YOU in whom I believe and depend so much upon?
He is my Savior, Lord Jesus Christ, the Father and the Son
He is my Comforter, Protector, my Creator and my Confident
Who once again, on this earth, He will assent
Until then I know He will not put upon me more than I can bear
Whatever I do, where ever I go, I know He will be there
Some days I feel that I have let Him down
But, I just reach out and I know that He is around
No matter how one says it, or how it is defined
YOU are never late, YOU are always on time

Marlene Wheeler Scott

A Childs' Prayer

I watched as this young boy came to the altar today
And my heart broke as I heard him Pray
Dear God, I am not asking this for me
I am asking this for my Mommy and my Daddy
Please touch them and heal their pain
I want them to come back to church with me again
God, I know that you know just what they need
And God, you can use me to help plant the seed
You gave me to them to give them happiness
And I really am trying to do my best
Every day I give them a hug and say "I love you"
Then wait for them to say that they love me too
His head still bowed as he arose
I saw his tears as down his cheeks they flowed
God, please cradle him In Your arms when he goes to bed tonight
Let him know that you heard his prayer, things will be alright
For you said that the little children will suffer not
And God, I know this child you have not forgot

This little boy did come to the altar that Sunday and prayed for his parents I was sitting close to him and I heard his prayer to God.

A Cry for Help

Heavenly Father, I heard a friend cry out today
And for her too, I want to pray
Lord, she has overcome so much strife
In her constant struggle within her life
Loved ones she has lost
It has not been without some cost
God, do not let her retreat into the past
Where she once thought she had found love that would last
For you have told us, the past has gone away
You are only promised this day
Yes, it is the future for which we now know we must live
And the promise of each day, that you give
My friend is a woman of strong faith
And she knows that if she will only wait
That Your promise to her for love and happiness
Will become a Reality and not just a Guess
She tells others that she knows she must be strong
That God is going to answer her prayer, it won't be long
We all have had pain that has broken our heart
But, it is our pain and how we heal that sets us apart
Apart, not from the feelings of each other
But, in the way that we each choose to recover
God gave to each of us, a mountain to climb, it was steep
But, with that climb He gave us memories to keep
So God, please, as my friend, that mountain she continues to climb

Marlene Wheeler Scott

Please, reach out and give her a sign
To let her know that You are there
Holding her hand and that You care
God you tell us to come to you with POSITIVE EXPECTATIONS
This prayer I know You will answer, with NO HESITATION.

A Day at the Beach

There was no school today and Royce was very excited, hoping
that this would be a big day for him...He jumped out of bed, ran
downstairs, saying, "Mommy. Mommy, can we go to the beach today
so I can swim and play and build sandcastles?" I lis Mother said
"no", because it looks like it is going to rain,
so we will have to wait and see.

Royce ran outside and looked up at the sky and all the dark clouds..
Oh please Mr. Sun. please come out so that I can go to the beach
today and play....Suddenly, Mr. Sun peeked through the clouds,
it was so beautiful and yellow and Royce got very excited
Mr. Sun, beamed down on Royce and said, "You
get your Mother and go to the beach
and I will hold back the clouds and the rain...I
will be at the beach waiting for you and I
will even come out and watch you play."

Royce ran back inside the house hollering,' Mommy, Mommy,
it is not going to rain, please, can we go to the beach?" "Alright"
said his Mother, "but, if the Sun does not come out or it starts
to rain, we will have to come back home", so, they loaded up the
car and headed toward the beach....His Mother said, "Royce, the
clouds look dark and the sky looks gloomy", but, Royce just smiled,
for he knew that Mr. Sun promised him he would be there.

Marlene Wheeler Scott

When they got to the beach, Royce jumped out of the car and ran to a big sand pile, then, be hooked up and there was Mr. Sun beaming down on him as if to say. "Enjoy your day little one, I will stay with you until you are ready to go home."

Moral:...Believe...If you Believe, then ALL things are possible

A Day in the Life of a Quarter

Hi!..My name is Quart, that is short for Quarter....I have the busiest day of anything and everyday is full of change... it seems like I am on the go all of theme.. Let me just tell you what the day in my life is like
Well, when I wake up in the morning, the first thing someone does is to pick me up and put me in their pocket... There I then meet Mr. Penny, Mr. Dime, and Ms. Nickle, all of them wondering where they are going and where they will end up at the end of the day
Before long, someone buys a drink at a store, they hand me over and I get put into a drawer with other change... there I will lay, but not for long, because suddenly, I get picked up and given to someone else who then puts me into their pocket, but before he does, for some reason, that person thinks he can flip me around in the air, boy, was I ever glad when he finally put me into his pocket, I was getting dizzy.
All day, I keep going to different people, until finally, I get put down for the night, in a safe place, the night stand next to his bed...I guess he wanted to make sure no one got me....Then, the next morning when he woke up, he scooped me up, put me in his pocket and now, the day will stand all over again
I do not know where I will go, what I will be used for, or, who will end up with me at the end of the day...Whatever and whoever, it will not be with the same spender, so, I guess this is why they call me ....CHANGE.

Marlene Wheeler Scott

A Joyous Celebration

I cannot, nor will ever forget this date
I promise that every year, for you a cake I will bake
Then I will light the candle, for I have no doubt
I will feel this small puff of wind, coming to blow it out
Parties, you always did love and could not resist
But, this special one, I know you will not miss We
will all be there, holding each other's hand
Waiting for the Angels to say, "Strike up the Band"
For we are all here today with your beloved brother
Celebrating this special day in Heaven with his Mother
Then, we will all join in together as we all say
"We love you Garry Lee, remembering you on this your Birthday
On earth today, you would have been sixty-four
But in Heaven now, you will be given many, many more

Garry Lee
We know that it has only been one week
And there are many questions we are asking, answers we seek
One thing we know, from us you hid your true pain
Never believed in carrying an umbrella when it rained
For you believed that God was washing
your body, cleansing your soul
Being in Heaven one day was always your goal
You worked hard, you always kept your Faith
In your heart you knew, time was important, no time to waste
Then, when the time did come, God gave to you
Times to say to loved ones and do the things you wanted to

Your brothers and sisters, they came from everywhere
To spend time with and visit with the brother they so loved and cared
You got to see and say to each of our family Things
you remembered doing with them, especially Things
so important as a family, you did together
All because we had a strong and loving Mother
Then, God, felt your pain, He came down to take you home
But, as your last wish, God did not let you die alone
Your beloved sister Mary was there to hold your hand
In peace, you then closed your eyes and
went home to the Promised Land
Yes, we will grieve for you and we will cry But,
there is one thing that none of us can deny
To each of us, you were such a special part

Of each of our lives, memories of you forever in our heart
Rest in Peace, our brother, Garry Lee, no more pain
God says we will all one day have a 'special Wheeler reunion' again

Garry Lee Wheeler
9/29/1951---9/20/2015

A Mother Makes the Family

A Mother will face many a trial
While trying to raise her beloved child
But of all the jobs, there can be no other
That has the joys and rewards than that of being a Mother
She gets no pension, nor can she ever retire
Her job is guaranteed, she cannot even get fired
From the moment that her child is born
She will never leave them, even when she gets tired, grows old or worn
She tends to her child through all their years
Leaving with them memories of laughter, joy and tears
Yes, a home may have a Father, a sister and a brother
But, it is not a family unless there is Mother
Mother, when I too grow and have a family
I pray for all the those things you instilled in me

A Star is Born
Number one

I learned a long time ago to be
A friend to others, but first to me
For whatever in my life that choose to do
It is I who must decide my life, not you
Because only I could walk in my shoes
So it is the choices I must choose
My decision should be my very own
It should not be brought into another's home
Friends are important, it is true, and for those who care
When called upon or needed, they are always there But,
if I take care of me, number one
Then, I can feel the victory for whatever I have done
No whispers or pity or saying, "I'm sorry about that"
To those who do not know or have all the facts
They fill their own life with so much misery
Trying hard to see what faults they can find in me
I have learned that life is given to us in different stages
The role we play improves as the player ages
We can either be the STAR while in this role
Or keep waiting for a CUE, doing what we are told
I want to be ready to walk off the stage through the door of eternity
I want to be given that Star that is awaiting me
A new role for me I will then embrace
When with the one who made me, I come face to face

Marlene Wheeler Scott

So, when I walk off this stage of life, and what is waiting for me
    Through that door onto the stage of eternity
    A new star will be born and will shine bright
    Forever, in the skies, lighting up the night

A Thankful Heart

The little deeds so thoughtfully done
The favors of friends and the love that someone
Unselfishly has given to us in so many ways
Was done because of friendship, not just to get praise
You were like a sister, my best friend, one of a kind
Forever, will you remain my heart and mind
For you have been my joy, seventy-years of living
Sharing with each other so much and to each, always giving
There comes to mind about a certain flower
That would also, forever be remembered in this hour
God was in His garden, giving the flowers each a name
When one flower said, Lord, I am ashamed
The name that you gave to me I have forgot
And the Father kindly said, "FOR-GET-ME NOT"
Joy, you are very much like that flower to me
Two friends, a friendship that was meant to be
Joy, I do not say "good-bye", I know that you are at peace
Your pain, and suffering have now all ceased
You are now in God's Garden, with the others you have now met
Know I will always remember you, I will never forget
So many memories of you l have got
You are my pick of the flowers, a FOR-GET-ME NOT

WRITTEN FOR A FRIEND OF MINE, BARBARA HARTER UPON
THE LOSS OF A DEAR FRIEND OF OVER SEVENTY-YEARS

Marlene Wheeler Scott

A Very Special Gathering Remembered

I want to say to one and to all
Thank you for this day, I will forever recall
Just seeing loved ones and family, some just met
Believe when I say, these wonderful people, I will never forget
Getting to meet new ones, heard about, now finally get to see
All a part of or getting ready to join our family
Rick Nelson, Pattie said that you were a pure delight
For once, I have to admit she is right
Jason, right away, just one hug and I knew
The right man, my granddaughter did choose
You even took the times to talk to me
About the possibility of getting a job for my grandson Steve
Michael and Dallas, both of you was happy to see
Celebrity parents of a Facebook star, which I call my T.V.
She is so adorable and you keep us all updated and informed
On her weekly growing, what she is doing since she was born
Another one, wow..so long since I seen you, Mindy Sue
You looked great, so good to hug and again see you
I met a beautiful lady, her name is Ashley
M y grandson Johnny has good taste, it is plain to see
Kyle was there, his Mother too
It was good seeing and talking to both of you
M y grandson Royce, he could not be there
He was working on Sullivan, or somewhere
But, he called, talked to me later on
Thank you Royce, you are a very caring grandson
Yes, I was so happy that today l was a pan
Of this special party, leaving memories forever in my heart

So many were there who wanted to share
And to be a pan of this special, saying they all really cared
Why was this day so special, I will give you the 'scoop'
But first, I have to divide them all into groups
First and foremost, it was for K.J.
Everyone came out to help him celebrate his birthday
His mommy Brittany any Jason wanted the family all together
When they announced to K.J. And Braylon,
they were going to have a brother
Then Ashley and Brandon, they too wanted to reveal
And to share their emotions and how they did feel
When they would reveal to everyone
If their first born was to be a daughter or a son
Congratulations were said to the proud parents

When the Ultra Sound came and made it quite apparent
That they were going to have a boy
Who would fill their lives with much love and joy
To all of you there whose names I did not mention
Just know, that in my heart, it was not my intention
For you all know that you are and will always be a part
Of my life and forever in my heart
K.J. I know that you bad an unforgettable day
In closing, there is more thing I want to say
To my daughter-in-law, Patti Scott
You were the perfect host thank you, love you a lot

It was my great grandson's birthday and also, my two granddaughters's REVEALING party, both having babies, within weeks apart....Both had sons.

ALL I WANT
{to my children}

I want no flowers, no jewelry, none of that stuff
That some think in giving is thanks enough
You can buy me a new outfit, yes, you could do that
Even add to the outfit a new pocketbook, shoes, and hat
Or, you could send me on a much needed trip
Maybe even a cruise, across the ocean on a ship You
could take me to a movie {I may have already seen}
Take me out dancing, called making the scene

All these things are nice and in good taste
But for me, it is money spent, almost a waste
For all I want Is for you to find time to spend with me
Come by for a visit, have dinner, or a cup of tea
To give me a hug, a kiss, to just keep in touch Tell
me you love me, now is this asking too much?
Today, I will be sitting by my telephone
To get that call, saying, "Mother, I'm on my way home"
Put the coffee pot on cause I am on my way
To spend time with you, this Mother's Day.

America Welcomes You

We believe in helping our fellow man
We believe in doing all that we can

We believe everyone deserves the chance To
better their lives, their futures to enhance
But, we also believe that we have the right
To defend our country from all who might

Cross our borders, into our land with only one thing in
mind To cause dissention, hatred and mistrust in all
mankind But, it will not work here, for America is strong
You will be found out and sent back to where you belong

It Is true some really do want to start a new life

Free from fear, threats, prejudice and strife
So, they sneak across our borders, trying to get in

In hopes of a new life they want to begin

It Is only the ones who want to rob and kill That
causes the people to say "we've had our fill". Then
our wanting to help them turns to hate Demanding
we send them back before it is too late Yes our
country is open to all who want to be free But we
will not let you take away our Liberty.

Marlene Wheeler Scott

ANGELA

The aches and pains, oh how our hearts cry
When a loved one leaves suddenly, no chance to say "good-bye"
Then we find ourselves all gathering together
Trying to understand and to comfort each other
Angela left behind a daughter and a son
She was so proud of them and what they had become
She also left behind a brother, Donnie, she loved him so
Although at times, she found it hard to show
Angela was a person who was very loving and caring
She did not have much, but she was always sharing
The birth of her grandchildren was the highlight of her life
They gave to her much love, made her forget a lot of her strife
Although Angela knew she was loved by many
She still fought demons she felt had become her enemy
She truly fought hard, wanting her pain to cease
Crying out for help and praying to God to give her peace
Angela was very, very close to her Mother Faye
And it left a void in her life when her Mother passed away
Angela, God has now given to you the peace you asked for
He is now uniting you with your Mother that you so adored
Though all your loved ones here are now crying out
For answers that has left them with so much doubt
You will be missed Angela, memories our hearts will retain
And know that a part of you in all generations will now remain
We are all comforted to know that you are now at peace

Peace you prayed that one day God would let you reach
We know your Mother Faye will be standing at Heaven's Door
Her arms outreached saying, "my daughter,
welcome, you will suffer no more."

Ann Ziegler

Ann, the campground has all come together
To say we are all saddened, bearing of the loss of your brother
From the very first day of his birth
God knew how long he would be upon this earth
God gave to him, brothers and sisters, who became a part
Of his life and he loved them with all his heart
Then God gave to him a wife a family of his own
life felt so blessed, watching them as they all became grown
From his home town of Elloree, he then moved away
But an illness brought him back and he prepared for this day
Ann, today as you all gather together
To say goodbye to a beloved husband. Father and brother
You will know that he will forever be in your heart
and in each of you, he will always be a part
You, John, Jarrod's family are all in our Prayer
Know that all here at the Campground loves you and we care
We want to let you know that if there is anything that we
can do As you have been here for us, we are here for you
God Bless you, each and everyone
In Jesus name, Thy will be done

ANNETTE

Annette, Annette. Annette
I made sure that my alarm was set
Because I sure did not want to miss
Sending to you a very SPECIAL WISH
I know that you will have lots of fun
Celebrating with family, friends and loved ones
Annette, in your own wonderful way, so many you have touched
That is why we all love you, very much
But, know that this is not the only day
That we all take time for you and to say
That we all love you, yes we do
Just because you are special, you are you
Everyone has gathered round you so we could all say
We love you Annette!!!! HAPPY BIRTHDAY!!!!!

Marlene Wheeler Scott

Aunt Joyce

Sometimes we do not get a chance to say 'good-bye'
And only God knows the reason why
Why He chose this special loved one to call home
Leaving a void here, her loved ones feeling so alone
Aunt Joyce was a special, much loved, yes indeed
She was witty, charming, always had a surprise up her sleeve
She had the most beautiful smile
When she smiled at you, you felt special, made you feel worthwhile
Joyce also bad a beautiful daughter, her name was Bobby Jo
Like Mother, like daughter, you could feel their love flow
Bobby Jo gave to her a grandson, Anthony
She was as proud of him as she could be
He was her everything, he was her 'pet'
She was his MaMa, who he will never forget
Joyce had a brother who earlier had passed
Leaving a void and grief, for her that would forever last
Two brothers she had, Jimmy and Johnny....she dearly loved
But her heart still ached for her brother above
Suddenly, her beloved husband Mike, God took home too
She felt such a void, not knowing what she was going to do
Though she tried hard to put on a 'happy face'
Her heart was heavy, she felt she was in a race
She knew her God, and she often talked to Him
And one day she said, "God, only You will know when"
My journey here will over, when I must leave
But, I do not want my loved ones to grieve
For I know that I will again see my husband and beloved brother

And we will soon embrace each other
Though my journey here will be over, do not cry
We will see each other again…this is not good-bye
This journey in my life, God has closed
But a new life, He showed me He has chose
A new life on earth that had just began
A beautiful baby girl, my niece, Finley Ann

GOD SAYS, "EVEN IN DEATH, LIFE GOES ON"

Because of You

I am Blessed and privileged to be a part
Of a special, mild mannered man who has touched so many hearts
Whenever help was needed, he was there, extending his hand
Saying, "tell me what you need, I will do whatever I can"
He was so happy he could help, but always gave God the praise
For choosing him to spread God's love in so many ways
He spent his time with friends, loved ones, strangers too
But, as he grew older, he felt his times were becoming all to few
Although he has a loving family, he still felt alone
Since the day that God called his beloved Josephine home
He filled his days feeding the homeless, doing for others
Spreading God's word of love and peace to all his Sisters and Brothers
Now, he too has become tired and he has reached out his hand
To God, saying, "God, I have finished, take
me home to the Promised Land"
But, I know God replied, "yes, I know that you are ready to go
But, when I am ready, I will let you know"
So God, I pray that You will reach down and touch
This man of God, we have all come to love so much
In the name of Jesus Christ, our Savior and Lord
Please, watch over and touch my friend, JOHN WARD.

God Inspired The Best in Me

Before the Storm

Sometimes we do not see the storm coming
When it confronts us, our instinct is to start running
But, we know that we must stand and face
The eye of the storm, because we have faith
Faith that in the end, the storm leaves no harm
After the storm is over and there is peace and calm
Yes, we can ride a small storm out
Because of your faith, and your love leaves no doubt
That the next 'eye' you both will face and look into
Will be each others, saying, "I still love you"
Just remember that in any type of "stormy weather"
You can always get through it when you both stand together

After the Storm

Even after the storm has passed/cleared
Some things have taken it's toil as feared
But, God has put us both together
That takes importance over all other
He also gave to us a family
Which without Him, this would never be
But, even with a family, we sometimes feel alone
That makes us want to get out and roam
But, the loneliness seems to still be there
I feel guilty for forsaking those I love and for whom I really care
I went back to a life of partying and what I called fun
A life that after I met you, that I had shunned

Marlene Wheeler Scott

It was because of you that I had given it up
Now, it is back again, my life it will disrupt
I now feel even more alone
I miss you, my family and my home
For no matter how much this other side looks like fun
When the day is over and all is said and done
I sit alone, in shame I hang my head
Because of what I have done and this life again let
I want you back, I want my family
I know now just how much you all meant to me
I have asked God to forgive me for what I have done
I have forgiven you, but I am not the one
For it is not Me you now must prove yourself to

It is to all of those who still love you
So, I am asking you from the bottom of my heart
Let me come back to where I was once a part
Part of a family who loved me for what I was
Never questioned me and never judged
Yes, the most important thing, above all the other
Is that we are again a family and will soon be together
We are a close family and with each other we belong
Then all will see that our love is still very strong

written for a friend whose husband tell her for another woman, leaving her with four children and became a man with a lot of remorse and regret,,,,it is he who must find his way back and pray that it will not be too late

God Inspired The Best in Me

Bonita Griffin

I heard this was going to be a very special day
And lots of good things were headed her way
This special lady that we all have come to know
One that we have come to respect and love so
She is her own person, speaks her mind
She is a special friend, she is one of a kind
A loving wife and a great Mother
Soon to be blessed by becoming a grandmother
Bonita, you are special and yes, by far
You deserve this day, today you are the star
Bonita Griffin, I join with so many others to say
I love you Bonita, God Bless and!!!HAPPY BIRTHDAY!!!

written for Bonita Griffin, wife of our Pastor, Kenny Griffin
for her September, 2015 birthday

BONITA

The words are truly hard to find
To express to you at this time
You have felt heartache and much blame
Feeling your life would never again be the same
But Bonita, know your loved ones have felt your pain too
Wanting to help carry your burden because they love you
Your faith in God has taken you this far
You will make it, you are strong, yes you are
Bonita, I would just like to say
As you remember your loved ones today
Your cousin Kevin and Earl, your brother
Just remember that they are now both together
Together in a place we too one day want to be
Forever with God in Eternity

**OUR PASTOR'S WIFE WHO BURRIED HER BROTHER
AND WATCHED HER COUSIN DIE IN A CRASH
ALL WITHIN HOURS OF EACH OTHER**

Written for Bonita who lost both her brother Earl Miles and her cousin Kevin within A few days of each other...Dec. 2012

CAMDEN....CLASS REUNIONS
June 27th, 2015

So many classes, tonight have gathered here
Classes gathered to remember yesterday, looking forward to next year
For us, we were the "CLASS of 55"
The class, no matter the obstacle, we would survive
We were a small class, thirty of us
Over the years, we have all stayed in touch
We had so much fun while in school
I think of our class as being "REALLY COOL"
Many memories we have, each of us having our own
Memories that have stayed with each of
us, no matter where we roamed
Sadly, some of our classmates have passed and are greatly missed
Here are the names on our memory list:
Joe Willeford, Ronnie Barnett, Richard Kiracofe, Gordon Keller
Roger Flora, Marvin Robertson, Connie Wysong,
Josephine Creech Mary Ann Mann
With us also, but not on our graduation day was,
Raymond Dill and Donna Jean Suman
All of them were and still are very much a part
Of our Class of "55", forever in our heart

Marlene Wheeler Scott

My name is Marlene Wheeler Scott and I am so
proud to say that I went to Camden High
School, graduating in 1955...I feel honored to have
gone to Camden High School during
this time and to have been under the teachings
of so many of whom I learned so
much....such as Robert Davies, William Browning,
Ms. White, just to name a few
My senior class was very special to me...We were
close then and here, sixty years later,
we still remain close and keep in contact with each other
After graduation, I moved away and later in my
years, I persued a dream of mine, to
write, and wiith Faith in God and with God giving
me the words to write, I have written
several books of poetry and children's books
which have been published...So many of
my poems have been written for, or about my
classmates, family and friends...My
classmates and my church are a large part of my
poems...I feel honored to have been
asked to write special words for them..
My family moved to Camden when I was in the fifth
grade...I have a lot to be thankful for, and one of them is
thanking God for having sent my Father and family to
CAMDEN...MY HOME TOWN.

God Inspired The Best in Me

Camden..My Home Town

There is much that can be said about a small town
Things like, everybody knows everyone around
Not only that, but they know everything about everyone
Even to what they are doing and what they have done
But, one thing for sure, if you need help, they are right there
Not because they have to, but, because they care
In this farming community, farmers work hard for their crop
But if someone is in need of help, they will stop
Stop to help them out, whatever the need
Even to help planting a fellow farmers seed
I hold memories of our school, one, our paper drive, it was great
Helping to raise monies needed for our Sr.
Class trip, we could not wait
I remember this being special because they paid for a classmate to go
Yes, they paid so she could go, it was me, so I should know
This is just one of the memories of how everyone goes out of their way
To help out others, no matter the need, on any given day
This is a town that stands together
Never too busy to find time for each other
To me, Camden has such a beautiful sound
Camden, the place I call, MY HOME TOWN
CAMDEN
This is the place I love, it means so much to me
My home town, Camden, in Preble County
Where everyone, when walking down the street
Never a stranger will they meet
On Sunday mornings the church bells will ring

In all the churches, you can hear the people sing
They sing of their blessings, and give praise to God above
Thanking Him for His Blessings and His love
Then the streets all become quiet at this time
For everyone has only one thing now on their mind
It is to have a day of worship; with their family and friends
Feeling Blessed, but sad when the day finally ends
Yes, this is the place I again long to be
Camden, it will always be home to me
It is a small farming town
But a friendlier place cannot be found
CAMDEN....MY HOME TOWN

June 27th, 2015

Cousin Bonita Griffin

Bonita, if I could be there with you for a
moment, not only so I could say
But to hold you and tell you, I too wish I could have changed that day
You have kept this guilt for so very long
But, I know that it is your Faith and prayers
that are keeping you strong
You were not the cause of what happened to me
I know you are finding this so hard to believe
But, just like so many have blamed Lynette for Earl's death
It was God, not Lynnetewho took Uncle Earl's last breath
So too, just like the motorcycle that I chose to jump on and go riding
It was God who was then deciding
Upon how I would that day meet my fate
It was God's decision, not yours to make
I am now at peace and I understand and I now know
That all the old memories I had, I had to let go
So too should you Bonita, though that day changed your life
You were still Blessed at being a Mother and a loving wife
God would soon be blessing you with a beautiful granddaughter
She had been your wish and prayer and God had not forgot her
Now Bonita, there is so much to her you have to give
Enjoy your time together and LIVE
Do not let these memories of yesterday haunt you anymore
You and Pastor Kenny have so much to live for
I know that your pain he too has felt and it has impacted him too
But he believes in and loves his God, and he believes in and loves you
Remember that I too left a family, sons, a daughter and a wife

Marlene Wheeler Scott

My passing also changed their future and their life
My Mother and brothers are all still trying to understand
I see my Mother in tears, coping with all
her losses the best way she can
Yes, life indeed changed for so many that day
Each one hurting, each one in their own way
Nothing or no one will ever be the same
But, by believing and living your lives, you honor my name
Just remember, my dear cousin Bonita Griffin
The good times we had together, yes, them I am a 'missin'
You and Kenny continue to go on and enjoy your cruises
Just remember, we will all be together again,
but not before God chooses

I wrote this for a wonderful friend who, in one day laid her brother to rest and seen her cousin Kevin killed and put her into deep depression...it has been three years

Cousin's Day

Cayden woke up, rubbed his eyes, sat up in bed and looked all around his room....Everything seemed to be there and still in place... Cayden had dreamed that someone came into his room while he was sleeping and took some of his games and toys, but, everything was still there, so, Cayden knew he had just had a bad dream.

"Oh boy" Cayden said as he jumped out of his bed…I smell breakfast and it smells really good....So, he ran downstairs into the kitchen, and there was his Mother fixing his favorite breakfast, pancakes and bacon.....His Mother turned and smiled at him, gave him a big hug and kiss and told him to have a seat at the table, his breakfast was ready.

After they were finished eating, Cayden's Mother told him to go upstairs and get dressed while she did the dishes, that she had a surprise for him and they were going to have a very busy day....Cayden got excited, but, he asked his mother if he could help her with the dishes...She told him no, and thank you but, you can do the dishes tomorrow.

After they got into the car, Cayden turned to his mother and asked her where they were going...His mother said, "Cayden, today we are going to visit your cousins, Maddox and Grayson, then we are all going to go to the park to let you all swing and play, then, we are going to the Zoo where you can see all the animals and then we are going to go to your favorite place to eat and get hot dogs and french fries and a chocolate shake"....."Oh

Mother" said Cayden, "you are the best Mother in the world...I love you so much" and he gave her a big hug and a kiss.

His Mother said, "This is going to be a special day and we are going to do this once a month and we will go to different places and do different things...These will be days that you boys will remember always, and we are going to call it Cousin's Day, so, Cayden, Maddox, Grayson and all their Mother's started off on this adventurous day with their sons...They went to the most wonderful places, they saw the monkeys, the lions and the ducks in the pond at the park, they slid down slides, went swinging on the swings, even played some tag with each other, then, they all went to eat hot dogs, french fries and drank milk shakes.... All too soon the day was over and they all went back home.

That night, after Cayden's Mother heard his prayers and tucked him into bed, she leaned over, gave him a kiss good-night and asked him if he enjoyed the day and being with his cousins ....oh yes, said Cayden....I love my cousins and this just brought me closer to them and I had so much fun, "Mother, I am going to write the President tomorrow and tell him that everyone needs to have a Cousin's Day"..
His Mother smiled and said, "Now Cayden, that is a very nice idea"....Cayden, smiled, snuggled under his blanket and fell fast asleep...He knew he was going to have a wonderful dream tonight.

CREMATION

When I die, I do believe and I know
That God will have taken my Soul
The flesh that was given to me in birth
Will return to dust when I am returned into the earth

Loved ones can choose to tote me around
Or bury my body deep into the ground
Because when God comes to take me and my Soul
He will then give me a new body and He will make me whole

God made us all from the earth and clay
And He made us all, in His own way
He gave us a body of flesh, then He made us whole
By giving each of us a Soul

So, when I die, it is your decision that must be found
Of whether to bury me or spread my ashes around
God said that from ashes to ashes and dust to dust
One day we will all return - this is a must

So, my decision is made and you all know
What to do with me when I go
So, whatever you feel to do within your own heart
Nothing that is done, will keep us apart

Marlene Wheeler Scott

You can bury me, carry me, throw my ashes to the wind
Remembering my life with you and then
Take those memories, that will be all that will remain
'Til God brings us all together again.

Crying Out

Lord hear my cry and hear my pleas
Open my eyes that l might see
I have been blinded for so long
I was weak, but God, please make me strong
Somewhere I began to lose sight
Of others feelings, thinking that only I was right
I did not have time if someone needed help
I did not care about how they felt
Just thinking, it was I who should come first
Not caring if anyone would be hurt
But, today, I dropped down on bended knee
My heart is aching from things I now see
Even though I had gone astray
Lord, you stayed with me, every day
You knew that I would be coming back
My faith in You, I no longer would lack
I asked you for a Miracle that could see
In one day, you gave me not one, but three
Thank you God for the blessings you have given to us
Blessings everyday, you have given, I love you so much
Now, when I awake each and every day, I will say
"Thank You God, thank You for another day"

Marlene Wheeler Scott

Dangerous Woman

When I awake in the early morning, still not feeling rested
I get the feeling that my day is going to be tested
But before you begin to test me, especially one on one
Just remember, I consider myself to be a 'Desperate Woman'

No one has ever called me weak
Because they know that if I should find myself up a creek
They know that I will make it back to shore
I am a 'Desperate Woman', I do not need an oar

People seem to always come to me
Especially whenever they feel they have a need
They know that I will get things done
Because, I am a 'Desperate Woman'

I know that I am not as young as I used to be
Whenever I look into the mirror and I see
Wrinkles that are starting to cover my face
I then know that desperate measures, I have to embrace

I do not give up easily, nor do I give in
I do not ask how, or question why, I only say, "when"
They know that desperate measures I may need to take
But, they know it will be done, make no mistake

Many children I have had in my life
I was a devoted Mother and a very good wife
But, as my children grew and began to leave home
In desperation I did things, because I was feeling so alone

But, now I am older and I have learned to be
A little less desperate, awaiting more patiently
Now doing things for me and what I think is best
A desperate woman, yes, I think I passed that test

Desperate Woman, I am still proud to be
Desperate Woman, yes, that is what they still call me
This Desperate Woman just wants to live her life and Pray
That this Desperate Woman gets to Heaven one day

Written for my friend Mary

Don't Take Away....My U.S.A

I heard the song, My Country tis of Thee
And I wondered, what was it's History
I felt like it was something that I should know
On how or what helped this country to grow
I learned it had been taken out of our schools
When a new Government began invoking new rules
Saying that the Old America was now in the past
New religions, immigration and illegals were growing fast
Making our jobs scarce and the money tight
Somehow, this new America does not sound right
We have to stand in long lines for our food and welfare
Being dependent upon a Government that doesn't care
They tell us the air to breath and the food to eat
Freedom of speech, they have even tried to delete
We cannot worship the God of our choice
We no longer have a voice
I also read that this was a country that once did care
They were willing to welcome all Legals and to share
Share with them the opportunity and freedom they too had
But, this was all taken away, how very sad
I want to go back to that Old Country
That was free, and in God they believed
I am willing to fight for all of this
And the freedom our generation has missed
My generation was never asked or given a voice
The New Government did not give us a choice
We now know what they did was so very wrong

God Inspired The Best in Me

But, we are becoming a Nation that is again strong
So, we will stand and yes, we will fight
For what we believe in and for what is right
This was a country who fought for all of us
Their power was felt the world over by all they touched
America will once again stand tall
Giving Liberty and Justice to all
GOO BLESS AMERICA...the land of the Free
AMERICA...MY COUNTRY TIS of THEE

FALL

This is the season when colorful changes one sees
Especially the foilage from the graceful trees
They stand so graceful and tall, their beauty we behold
They are a symbol of strength and long life, we are told
I stand in awe, just watching these trees
Swaying so gently, as they embrace God's breeze
Then, when the leaves begin to fall in Winter late
They become dormant, do not die, they begin to vegetate
Again to give back to the tree, food and nourishment
For this is why the leaves were sent
Their beauty and color giving us wonder and many smiles
Even though their time with us is only for a while
We can all learn so much from the trees
For each of us, it is in the eye of the beholder that we see
Just like the tree that has now lost it's leaves
We too have losses and we too will grieve
True, we cannot see God, but, we see Him in His beauty, every where
All He asks us to do is this growth and love, is to share
Though some think that these cycles of seasons are strange
Cycles too in life we will have, and we too will change
God is giving to us different seasons
To let us know that, if for no other reason
To let us all know that no matter what the weather
We become stronger when the seasons, all
different, brings us together.

Follow Your Heart

Have you ever felt in your heart that something was wrong
But could not talk to anyone, tried to stay calm
But, there was something you had gotten yourself into
Now, you wanted out, but did not know just what to do
You knew in your heart and without a doubt
You had to quickly, find a way out
The decision you made, you knew would hurt someone
You cried out to God, "what did I do, God what have I done"?
God said, "my child, I have heard your cries and I see your tears
I am here to answer your Prayer and calm your fears"
The answer you already know, it lies within your heart
The secret you have carried for so long, in the dark
To so many and to yourself you have lived a lie
A lie that you can no longer deny
Your eyes have now been opened and you can see
That you have come to terms with what now must be
Of this lie that you will no longer be a part
You will be free and a new life you will now start
I approve your decision, stay strong and do not back down
Remember and know, if you need Me, I will always be around.

Marlene Wheeler Scott

Friends Found—Friends forgotten

Sometimes we have the tendency to forget
People, who along our paths we have met
They came and walked that mile with us
But in time, they were forgotten we had lost touch
But, did it ever occur to you
That they may be wanting to find you too? We
had walked together, endured much wrath
But together, as friends we had learned to laugh
We gave each other strength and hope
We helped each other and we learned to cope
But now, we need each other again
For we have another battle, together we must win
So, stop for a moment, reach out your hand
Saying, "I am here for you, I understand"
Together we can again walk that road
And help to share each others load
The road may not be easy, but God will lead the way
Because we believe in Him and we must take the time to pray
He has again reopened that door
Bringing us all together once more
He will be waiting for us where that road will end
Showing us this new life, we will now begin
God has a reason for bringing us together
He said He knew, we must again be with each other
I'm so glad that we have found each other again
Welcome back home my friend

Naming My Friends

My friends names begin with A- ends in Z
Their ages range from one {1}, into their early nineties {90}
They are not too young and not too old
But all of them are worth more than gold
I know whatever my needs, I just need to call
I thank God for each of you, yes, one and all
I do not tend to tag or only name a few
Just know I know your name and in my heart I carry ALL of you

Garry Lee

To you my brother, I want to say
How fulfilling were these past few days
And the wonderful time that I have spent
Time with you Garry Lee, I cannot tell you how much it has meant
The love and strength that I see you emit
Is one that I will never forget
You were prepared for the challenge given to you
Because you knew your Faith in God would bring you through
Though the tunnel was long and very dark
It was a journey with God that you would embark
So, as you began to grow stronger, you kept moving ahead
Until out of the tunnel you came, knowing it was God who led
Yes, the tunnel was long and dark, but God was there
Always by your side, because He cared
So, I thought I would take a little of my time
To write to you, a few words in rhyme
To let you know just how much
You are loved and so many lives you have touched
Not only to me, but to so many others
I am so proud to call you my 'brother'
There are three little words not said often enough
Because some [especially] men, calls it 'mushy stuff'
But when they are spoken from the heart, then it is clear
The words are indeed, very sincere
So from my heart, I want to want very much to say
Garry Lee, "I LOVE YOU", not just today, but every day

MY BROTHER, GARRY LEE WHEELER
BORN SEPT. 29, 1951
PASSED AWAY SEPT.20.2015

God Did Not Change

Evil is lurking everywhere
And it is becoming more than I can bear
According to the news and the paper
Our daily lives are still no safer
Some go to church so that they may pray
While others just shrug it off and say
That it is our young folks and that it is just a trend
They will soon grow up and this will all end
But, we cannot blame it on the young alone
The responsibility belongs to us, we have brought on
We have watched drugs run rampant, slowing our teens brain
Making the do things that are crazy and so insane
Even the gays are now openly saying that it is okay
That they are the new generation and it is becoming the new way
But, ever since the very beginning of time
When murder, the Bible speaks of being the first crime
The disobedience of Adam and Eve in the Garden back then
Denied their creator God, causing our first sin
But, God's Laws spoken to all are still the same
It is, that you obey His Law and Praise His Name
He says we must be ready and be free from Sin
For He will return to judge, we just do not know when
We must all be prepared for that Judgment Day
We cannot wait until He comes, than ask Him for time to Pray.

God Knows When We Need Someone

Sometimes words are just never enough
And a 'thank you' does not sound like very much
For someone who seems to be forever there
Not as a have to, but because they truly care
I found myself in a dilemma, not knowing what I was going to do
She was right there for me, saying, what can I do for you?
Whatever you need, you only need to ask
But it is God who will lift your burdens, they will not last
She is there if I just need to talk
She is there if I want someone to go with me for a walk
She is there for a quiet cup of coffee or a sip of tea
She is always there for others not just for me
I do believe that God sends to all of us
Someone that knows when to reach out and to touch
The ones who are grieving or in need
I believe that God sent that someone to me
I only pray that if she too should one day
Need help, I can say, my friend, I am on my way
She, during my lifetime, will forever be
A friend in whom I have trusted and believed
As I said, words and a 'thank you' can never be
Enough for the friend that you have been to me
I want all to know you and so I say out loud
Shirley Fryer, you are a friend of whom I am so proud
Thank you and God Bless you forever more
I know God's reward awaits you, when one
day you enter through Heaven's Door

Marlene Wheeler Scott

God Will Say 'When'

No one can predict the day or the hour
For only God holds that kind of power
In Life, we seem to ignore the signs He gives to us
We just laugh them off saying, "He's an easy touch"
They say He is a forgiving God, that He will keep His word
But, is it His word that they have really heard?
We are seeing our friends, both young and old
Passing so quickly, never again will we be able to hold
We ask, "are they going to Heaven, or is it just in our Prayer?
That we pray when God took them, were they prepared?"
Should we then not look at our own selves
Asking God to pick us up if we should fall or fail
Are we living the life that God said we needed to
Or are we letting the Devil make us look like a fool?
Yes. God says our sins are forgiven, this is true
But, you must live a God given life til He comes for you
Stop going to bars, honky-tonks, trying to have a 'good time'
Saying to others, "you live your life and I'll live mine"
But those who love you and care are trying to say to you
These are the things that God does not want you to do
So please, listen to God's word my friend
Don't wait until God says, "today, this all will end"
I forgave your sins, I kept my word
All of your excuses, but no forgiveness, I have heard
The wages of sin is death, on this you can depend
Your time has run out, today I say 'when'

<u>I HAVE KEPT MY PROMISE AND MY WORD</u>

!!!!HAPPY BIRTHDAY!!!!-ALONICA & KERI
Dec. 09

It seems that two beautiful young ladies, on this date
Get to share a great, great big birthday cake
One of them is an Aunt, the other her Niece
But, I want to say to them each
You both have really, this old heart touched
And I love you both, very, very much
Keri, my beautiful granddaughter, now a new bride
Is celebrating her birthday with her new husband by her side
As you both blow out the candles and make a wish
Remember, it is your love for each other that will make you rich
Alonica, such a beautiful great-granddaughter
I cannot find enough words to say about her
She is beautiful, smart and so outgoing
Her love for people and for learning is so overflowing
She loves her Mother/Father, sister Kahleina too
She speaks in several languages, and really loves school
Today, you both have come together to celebrate
Your birthday, though born years apart, on the same date
So, we will now all gather around, no longer can we wait
To watch you both, cut into your birthday cake
Keri....Alonica....both of you we love and adore
HAPPY BIRTHDAY...and may God Bless you both with many more

Marlene Wheeler Scott

I Asked God, "Why Am I Here?"

I always wanted to have a good home
Filled with love and a family I could call my own
I wanted to serve God and do all His deeds
I asked Him to provide me with just my needs
God Blessed me with a loving home
God Blessed me with children I could call my own
God let me watch them grow into adulthood
I prayed to God that I did the best that I could
Then one day they all left, each found their own home
And God gave to them a family to call their own
God, children, grands and great grands You have given to me
Yes, You truly Blessed me with a wonderful family
Our gatherings, yes, we do make a wonderful crowd
All of them, I am so very, very proud
I thank you God for having given to me
Such a thoughtful and wonderful family
So, with pride to all of them I want to say
I LOVE you all, you are my life, you make my day

<u>MIKE/MARK/MELLISA/STEVEN</u>
<u>JOHNNY/BRITTANY/ASHLEY/ROYCE/CRYSTLE/KERI/TRESSA/TORI/STEVEN</u>
<u>BRIANNA/BLAKE/K.J./BRAYLON/MADDOX/</u>
<u>ALONICA/KAHLEINA/CAYDEN/GRAYSON</u>

<u>!!!WOW!!! WE NOW HAVE {2} MORE ON THE WAY</u>
<u>SO, WHAT MORE CAN I SAY?</u>
<u>EXCEPT THAT I LOVE YOU ALL SO VERY MUCH</u>
GOD WILLING, WHEREVER WE GO, MAY WE ALWAYS STAY IN TOUCH

God Inspired The Best in Me

I overcame/You can Too

I try hard not to think of what may have been
But of where I am now, where I am going and when
Living on the streets or in the slums
Is where some of our lives had begun
This is something which we did not yearn
When opportunities arise, grab it, don't wait your turn
I am now concentrated on me as number one
I am no longer a loser, I fought the battle and won
I now feel like a person, a living human being
I got my chance to be free and clean
Yes, some of my friends I have left behind
Our lives are separate but they remain on my mind
I wish them well and I truly pray
That they too find their future and will be okay
For me, I found God and I no longer have to hide or run
For I know that in God, all trials in life can be overcome

Marlene Wheeler Scott

ILLEGALS—
To what Country are you now loyal?

You sneak across our patrolled borders
Causing chaos within our own law and order
You cause anger and disruptions within our own land
Against those who vowed to protect us and to take a stand
You came across and then you laughed at us
Because you knew that we Americans are quick to trust
You say all you need to do is give us an "ole" sob story
And just pretend to love our flag, "Old Glory"
Yes, some of you do find work, but you take your money
From this, the country you call, the Land of Milk and Honey
And you send it back to help all of those
Who want to come here and of our laws dispose
Some say they are here let's give them their right and freedom to speak
Even if it is turmoil within our own country they really want to seek
But, freedom here in this United States does have a price tag
Especially when you trample on, burn, or disrespect our flag
Freedom of the Press and the ACLU
Does not speak for the majority, but only a few
Everyone cannot have it their own way
Here in our country, the good ole, US of A
I know If you were as verbal in your own land
And against your Government you chose to take stand
Then you would not need to cross our borders on the run
For you would be imprisoned, your nightmare will have just begun
So, do not bring us your problems, but we will pray
That you will find peace and live in your own country one day

God Inspired The Best in Me

IRENE

Irene, I just wanted to remind you and to let you know
That I truly, truly, did love you so
When we first met, I knew there would be no other
Even though some said that we should not be together
We married and we then became as one
You were my world, the moon, the stars, the Sun
Yes, God said this would always be, until death do us part
But, then, we would live on always, in each others heart
I can see your hurt and I can feel your pain
I hear you crying, wanting us to be as one, united again
Irene, you were the Mother of our children, my friend, my wife
You were my love and the reason for my life
When God called me home, He said He was not ready for you
For their was so much, still waiting for you to do
For our children's sake, you must stay strong
Teaching them about God and right from wrong
You too must now go on, and with another find renewed happiness
You have my blessing and my soul will be able to rest
For you are still young, so much for you still lies ahead
Do not live your life as though you too were "dead"
I love you Irene and I believe that you now know
We will always be together, in memory, in our heart and soul

Marlene Wheeler Scott

James Cline

When God designed and made man
He said, "I know that I can"
Create someone I know that will give
Hid dedication to Me, as long as he lives
He will be faithful, he will be true
His words and music will abound with you
So, on this day, October the first
A Mother will have given birth
To a son who will become known in time
All will know him as, James Cline
James, enjoy this, your God given day
You are loved and we have gathered here to say
God Bless you....!!!!!HAPPY BIRTHDAY!!!!

Jay Hodge
Aug. 30th, 2014

Today, the rain is pouring from the sky
Because so many tears today are being cried
Our hearts are aching, crying to be released
From this sudden loss that has befallen all of us
We are crying out of anger, hurt and pain
For a loved one suddenly taken, it is so insane
Losing a loved one we all love so much
Upon reality and time for us to adjust
To those fighting a battle, setting their own stage
Because of sickness and even from old age
But God, please help us to understand
What happened, why this young man?
He was so young and so full of life
To all who knew him, he was a pure delight
He loved camping, fishing, the great outdoors
Family gatherings, of which he thought there should be more
Two young sons, his pride and joy, he loved them both so
They were a part of his life, he loved watching them grow
It is so hard, so painful at the loss of a loved one
No parent can be prepared to suddenly lose their son
Jay was a son, a Father, cousin and a brother
Whose own life was just coming together
Jay's future here is over, but ours we now must face
As only the memories of Jay, we will now embrace
Jay, somewhere there is an answer as to why God took you away

Marlene Wheeler Scott

We all pray to find that answer one day
I think God had for you a much higher calling
He could not watch you keep falling
He knew that the word of God you had now found
And He took you while you were Heaven bound
Jay, God let you leave one last message that was loud and clear
To all your loved ones, especially the young ones here
That they still have time before it is too late
To come back in line with God, before you
suddenly too, will meet your fate
I apologize to all my friends and family, but God has forgiven me
If you stay in line with God, then one day in Heaven, we all will be

WRITTEN FOR HIS MOTHER DE-DE AND FAMILY

JENNIFER

Good morning Jennifer, how are you?
Today is going to be a good day, I tell you true
For you, there will be lots of Sunshine and lots of love
All surrounding you from Heaven above
Fair weather friends will come and they will go
But, in your heart, this you will know
You may have pain and you may hurt
But God is with you always, He will never desert
God will guide you from Heaven above
And He will surround you with all of His love
He will show you how to laugh and smile
Making your life living on earth, worthwhile
You have your family and you have your health
All the earthly riches, they call wealth
So smile, rejoice and sing God's praise
For He has blessed you in so many ways
If you got sad or when you feel blue
Then here is what you are to do
Lift your eyes to Heaven on High
Thank You God, I have no more need to complain or cry

This was written for a young lady who came to me and said that no one loved her.

Marlene Wheeler Scott

JERRY

I want to say Happy Birthday to none other
Than someone very special my brother
He has a wife, two sons whom he loves very much
Make sure his own family, they all stay in close touch
His brothers and sisters, he has eight
He also keeps us informed of all special dates
Our reunion especially, he looks forward to them
We would all be lost without him
My brother of whom we are all so proud
Is so special, he stands out in any crowd
He served his country, fougth in the Viet Nam War
He has scars, and relives those memories and much more
A prisoner of war, two medals, and a Purple Heart
Thank God, he returned home, a new life he would start
There is one part of his life however, he will never forget
His service to his country, dedicated, and now, a Viet Nam Vet
I want everyone to know how proud I am to be
Your sister, Jerry, thank you for putting up with me
So, keep us informed, updated and keep calling us
For, we know that with you, you will never let us lose touch
I love you Jerry and I want to say
I love you…God Bless you and !!!!HAPPY BIRTHDAY!!!!

God Inspired The Best in Me

Jessica

Jessica, God gave you to the one He knew
Would love you, teach you, and always take care of you
Ever since the day when to you she gave birth
She made sure that you would always come first
She watched over you as into adulthood you grew
But in her heart, she always knew
She could not always protect you from the things
That life and even mortals would sometimes bring
She also knew that in God's due time
She would have to leave you behind
She had so much pain, lots of hurt
She found solace and peace in her God and in her church
She wanted you to always know
That when you were in need, it was to God, to go
She loved you so much, but always felt in her heart
That there was something that was tearing you apart
Grandsons you gave her, of them she was so proud
She felt God had given her all the happiness that Heaven allowed
The times together that she and her grandsons spent
Passed so quickly, having so much fun, she
wondered where the time went
There was so much more that she wanted to do in life
Working for God, helping others, being a good Mother and wife
But, she knew that God was getting ready to call her home
Her only fear, was that of having to leave you alone
But, God spoke to her, gave her peace of mind
Saying, "your love for them, you will leave behind,

Marlene Wheeler Scott

They will carry on, for you showed them all bow to be strong
You taught them well, they know right from wrong"
So, when God called her hone that day
Your Mother said, "yes God, I am ready to go with You today,
For I have done all You wanted me to do, while here on earth
I am now ready for what I have awaited, my rebirth"

JESSICA, IEONA WAS ONE OF KIND…SHE LOVED HER GOD, HER CHURCH, HER FAMILY AND HER GRANDSONS' WERE TRULY A BLESSING TO HER…TELL THEM THAT SHE WILL BE WATCHING THEM IN THE SPORT OF FOOTBALL AND WHEN THEY GET THAT "TOUCHDOWN", SHE IS GOING TO BE CLAPPING HER HANDS, JUMPING UP AND DOWN, YELLING, WE DID IT, YOU HELPED ME TO REACH MY ….GOAL

JOHNNY

Feb. 9th, 1986

Johnny, you were my first grandson
When I first saw you, my heart, you instantly won
As I watched you grow into a fine young man
I quickly became your number one fan
I am so proud of you and what you have become
I thank God everyday for giving me such a fine grandson
The road paved for you has been very rough
You overcame these obstacles because you were determined and tough
You have in you, your Father's Genes
So much of him, in you I have seen
You had your dream, you fought hard to make it come true
You never gave up, you struggled, it says a lot about you
It made you work harder on that ladder you would climb
God was with you all the way, all the time
I love you Johnny, these words everyday I can say
But only once a year, I can say, !!!HAPPY BIRTHDAY!!!
So, !!!HAPPY BIRTHDAY!!! JOHNNY, my wonderful grandson
This is your God given day.....enjoy it...have lots of fun

Marlene Wheeler Scott

Joseph & Bubba
Bonded forever

This is the story of a young boy, when born was
called Bubba, and upon his birth, it changed the
lives forever, for him and his Uncle Joseph
Joseph became the babysitter for his sister Angela
and her family while she worked
Joseph wanted so much to be included in and to be a part
of his family and to help Joseph became attached to this
young boy Bubba, there was just something that drew the
Mo of them together...Joseph took extra good care of him
and helped him, watched him as he began to grow, being
there when he took his first steps and said his first word.

At night, Joseph would put Bubba down to sleep, but not before
reading to him and saying his prayers with him....One prayer
Bubba always asked for was that he would never be left alone,
especially in the dark....he always wanted to keep his light on, it
made him feel safe and secure...One night Uncle Joseph assured
him that God was always with him and that God sent him to watch
over him and that he was never going to leave him, that he could
turn off the lights at night because he would always be there, so,
Bubba awaited every night for Uncle Joseph to turn off the lights,
it was then he knew he would be okay and would fall asleep.

As Bubba grew older, be and his Uncle began spending a lot more time together...they would go fishing, camping, playing ball, playing video games in his room...His room had become a safe haven for him...It was in his room that Bubba and Uncle Joseph would sit for hours, talking, him telling his Uncle what was bothering him and then the two of them would discuss it and even have debates on some things...The two of them really loved their 'debates'.

Uncle Joseph was an artist in his own rights. and he was proud of the work he could do....He loved doing tattoos for those who asked....He also loved the outdoors and doing yard work, improving the yard in any way he could, even built a water well with lots of bricks and stones, and a fountain.

Bubba respected and admired his Uncle Joseph so much.... He said that his Uncle bad called him his 'Home Boy' and that home boys are strong and tough and always there when someone needed help....He said his Uncle taught him about having respect for others and to always keep a promise that be had made....He said a lot of people will judge you to your word and your modesty....He also told him that all of this would only be if he kept Jesus is his heart and did His bidding....

Bubba said that his Uncle Joseph told him one day that he felt that God had brought the Mo of them together for a reason...to watch over each other, to take care of each other and that he felt they had been good for each other....however, Uncle Joseph told him that

One day God was going to call him home, but, be wanted Bubba to know that he would still always be with him, he just needed to call his name.

One day, Bubba said he had left his room and overheard his Mother and family talking and crying...they came over to him, held him close and said, "Uncle Joseph is not coming back home, God has come and taken him to his Heavenly home....Bubba said he turned and ran back into his room....his safe haven....where they had spent so much time together and he wanted to feel his Uncle Joseph was still there.

Bubba went into a deep depression...be missed his Uncle Joseph so much, he kept his lights on, he could not turn them off and he even thought about suicide. For he felt then they would be together again....One night, he cried out, saying, "Uncle Joseph, where are you"? Suddenly he heard a very familiar voice saying, "Bubba, I have never I tell you, I have always been here...! have been watching you and waiting for you to accept what has happened and start believing and being strong....You have a long life ahead of you Bubba and you have so much to give, to be able to help some young boy one day, the same way I have helped you".....Bubba, you are going to be okay...I will always be here for you, to talk to you and watch over you as you say your prayers at night....Now Bubba, please, turn off those lights tonight before going to bed....l told you everything was going to be alright......So, Bubba and Uncle Joseph had their debate, and their talk, and Bubba felt a warm hug surround him, he stood up, walked over to the light and turned it off:...Yes, Bubba said, I am going to be alright....Uncle Joseph is still here.

God Inspired The Best in Me

Juanita Elizabeth Hall

God chooses the parents and also the home
Where His children will be loved and never feel alone
A beautiful daughter was being born to a loving Mother
A proud Father and a very excited and happy to be brother
Kandice herself was raised in a loving home and taught to be
Herself by answering to and obeying God, she would always be free
She was also taught by two loving Grandmother's she so respected
That it came as no surprise, something everyone had expected
That she would name her first daughter, her
first name she would be giving
To honor her Grandmother's and to keep
their memories forever living
Juanita and Elizabeth are both in Heaven sitting upon this cloud
Looking down on their granddaughter saying,
"Kandice, you have made us so proud"
Kandice sang in church with her father, listened
to her Uncle, Pastor Kenny preaching
She never forgot or refrained from her church or her teaching
True to God, her first born Joshua also would not be denied
She brought him home to her church, to be Baptized
Now, her second child, a daughter so very much loved
Was also brought home to her church and
Baptized with God's Blessings from above
Kandice and Jeremy, God is never, never wrong
These children He put where they both belonged
Knowing that you both would love them and teach them the way
That would prepare them, not for yesterday, but for today

Marlene Wheeler Scott

God's Blessings will continue to shine upon the both of you
This family who to God has remained Faithful and True

<u>Juanita Elizabeth Hall</u>

The daughter that they had been waiting for
Arrived weighing 6 lbs/12 oz, Sept. 17th, 2015 at 11:54

Keeping A Smile On Your Face

You try so hard to please so many others
You try to keep peace and bring everyone together
Even when you are hurting, it does not show
You just keep smiling, no matter where you go
But, a good friend can see behind that smile
Because we know you have a heart of gold, the love of a child
You are so trusting that some take advantage of you
Because you are innocent and forgiving, yes, this is true
Misguided and jealousy of some, they try to take you down
Dig you a grave, try putting you deep into the ground
Tell them, "ain't no grave gonna hold my body down
I will rise above them, I will hold my own ground"
For no matter the hurt, we know in our heart
You will keep striving, coming out in front of, not behind that cart
We all know that everyday will not be a bed of roses
But brings with it lots or uncertainties and supposes
But, you keep striving and keep that smile on your face
It tells others, you never gave up or gave in, you kept the Faith.

Marlene Wheeler Scott

Krystle & Charlton

With much anticipation, we did await
An event that would be so great
The birth of our little baby girl
Soon to enter into our world
Then, on July 11, in the early morn
Our beautiful baby girl was born
Our tears then quickly began to flow
As the Dr. told us, "she is not ready to go"
She has to stay with us just a little longer
Until she could become a little more stronger
God, you let me carry her for nine months
I know you will now carry us for this 'hump'
Even though our wait has been lengthened
Our Faith in You has only become strengthened
When we get to bring her back home
Know she will never be alone
Mom and Dad will always be by her side
Big brother will hold her, he will not be denied
Of course, Grandma/Grandpa/Aunts and Uncles too
Not counting all her cousins, nieces and nephews
So many baby sitters, when needed it will be hard to choose
We will have to mark on the calender when their day is due
God, we thank You so much and we are all so excited
Our little girl home, the word 'family' has been highlighted

Leona
My Eulogy to You

I write this in memory of someone who not only
had become my friend and a sister to
me, but to everyone that she met
She greatly touched our lives and our hearts with
her wit, her humor and her smile and
with her caring ways
She tried so hard to please, never wanting to be
a disappointment to anyone...She never
judged anyone, gave everyone a chance and yes,
even forgave a lot when she was hurt,
for she felt that this is what God wanted her to
do and by so doing, she showed others
that she truly was a woman of God and it was
from God that she got her strength
She held her friends in high esteem and her
family, there was no contest...She loved
them so much and was so proud of them....
She was proud that they followed in her
footsteps of going to church and always, always
trusting and believing in God, no matter
how bad or hard things sometimes seemed, know that God would
see them through it and tomorrow would bring a brighter day
I know she would say thank you to all and tell
them that even though the time with them

Marlene Wheeler Scott

may have seemed short, it was the time together
that was important...For there is no
greater gift that we can give to one another, than
to be aware of who they are and of their
existence....When they ask for help, do not
pretend that we do not hear them or see
them...reach out your hand
So, as she leaves loved ones and takes her next step
Just remember, her promise she has kept
My generation began with my children at birth
And while they too are upon this earth
As long as they keep God in their lives
This generation will continue to survive

Little Girl Lost

Jesus says He hears your cry, be feels your pain
He hears you trying to find someone to blame
So, when you decided that this was going to be your day
And from your home and teachings you would stray
So many lives you effected that would now take a turn
All because of an angry young girl who felt she had been spurned
You began having feelings, deep in your heart
That something was wrong, and it was tearing you apart
It all began a long time ago
Some things, you may never know
Yes, it all began at a time when no one wanted anything to do
With the responsibility of raising your brother or you
So, a woman of God stepped in, accepting you into her home
Along with your brother, so you would not be alone
Throughout the years of teaching, protecting and loving you
Some things she kept from you, yes, this is true
But, she never told you a lie or a falsehood
She was trying to protect you the best way she could
Your birth mother always knew where you were
But, from her, very few visits to you ever occurred
She would come to see you, the child she left go
Giving her false hopes, telling her things and that she love her so
Then, your adoptive Mother, watching her
leave and seeing your heart break
Became too much, it was more than she could take
So, she told your Mother, no more visits til she was willing
To take her home with her, her dreams of fulfilling

Marlene Wheeler Scott

You had dreams of living in a home with your Mother
Being a family, you, your Mother and your brother
Her neglect of you then caused anger, hurt and you began listening to
Lies about what happened now being told to you
Instead of this anger, you should be thankful to your second Mother
Who sacrificed much of her life, for the love of you and your brother
My child, I too have seen hatred, been lied about
Even spat upon by those, still in doubt
But, I forgave them, freely giving up my life for them
So their future would be brighter and not so dim
So did your second Mother who was willing to sacrifice
Doing whatever it took to give you a home, a good life
In this world so filled with hate, lies, and so much lust
It is hard to find that someone in whom you can trust

You should be thankful, you should tell
this woman that you appreciate
All she has done for you, and tell her before it is too late
You know, you too must ask for forgiveness and forgiveness receive
Before you can be whole and in your heart, find peace
Giving birth to a child does not a Mother make you be
Know that the woman who took care of you, was chosen by me
I know you are confused, you are feeling lost
But nothing in life comes easy, we all must pay a cost
You must learn to trust God and no matter what
Thank Him for the many blessings you have already got

LIVES MATTER
Black and White

All lives matter no matter what
And just in case you have forgot
It is really YOUR LIFE you should be caring for
You are the only one that can open that door
Why would you do or say something
That you know harsh words or conflict will then bring
Bringing with it a confrontation that could lead
To harm or death, because you did not heed
The warnings in some cases of breaking the law
Would bring punishment to one and all
The warnings that if the law you decide to break
Then, your being accountable, you cannot debate
So, stand up and be a man
Speak up, speak out, do whatever you can
To keep peace between us and among each other
Learn to get along, as sister and brother
This is your life and it should mean a lot
We should be free, we should not be bought
To do what a few would have us do
To keep turmoil going by a few
It is they who do not care whether you are black or white
They just want more power, to their delight
They do not care if our freedom thrives
They do not care about LIVES

Marlene Wheeler Scott

Take a stand, saying, enough, this has gone too far
You can make the difference, be proud of who you are
This is AMERICA, the land of the free
ALL lives matter, no matter the NATIONALITY

Memories of Joseph

I met Joseph a few years ago
A young man everyone called, 'TATOO JOE'
He had such a special talent, and as his reputation grew
He literally left his mark on all that he knew
I found Joseph to be a fine young man
Who wanted so much for people to understand
That although he had his faults, as we all do
His just seemed so much harder to get through
Out, in spite of his spats and outbursts that he had
It did not make him, as some said, bad
Joseph was talented, but he had a troubled soul
Who kept looking hard to find his goal
If Joseph promised to do a job you asked to be done
He would work hard, from Dawn to the setting of the Sunday
For it was his goal, it was his desire
That people would see his final work and admire
Except for the time that he fixed his Mother's car
Then took it for a test drive, but he did not get far
I remember a fish pond that he had built and designed
When completed, it was beautiful, it was one of a kind
A young woman told me of the most beautiful Butterfly
He had tattooed on her, yes, his talent could not be denied
Joseph just wanted to be treated with love and respect
Especially from those he loved, things he did expect
He wanted to be held, hugged and feel that special touch
Especially from his Mother, whom he loved very much
A Grandfather he respected and spoke so highly of

Marlene Wheeler Scott

But somehow, was never able to show or express his love
Nieces and nephews he had, and for them he loved to baby sit
It made him feel needed in the family he so wanted to fit
Though he loved them all, one stood out,
giving him so much pride and joy
His sister's son, "BUBBA", he was so proud of this young boy
Three loyal friends remained in his heart,
CLAYDIA, KIM and MISS IRENE
Always there for him, no matter what the need
To my sisters, Brittany and Angel, I just want to say,
I love you both very much, yes, we fought
a lot, but, it was just our way
Memories remained with me daily of my younger brother CHASE
I felt we were more than brothers, more like "SOUL MATES"
There was so much Joseph wanted to do and be
But, his young life was cut short so suddenly

I feel God looked down upon this troubled young man
Saying, "Son, I do understand'"
No longer all this pain and suffering you can endure
I have forgiven all, and your heart is now pure
No more worries will you have, you are safe from all harms
Your Grandmother is awaiting you in Heaven with open arms
To give to you that hug and that special touch
That you remembered and longed for so much
I truly believe that Joseph is now happy, and be would say
"Mother, I finally did it my way"

Mother
Sept. 23, 2015

Mother, when I was growing up, still so very young
You told me, "in life, always stand your ground, from it never run"
But, you never told me what I should, or had to do
Or try to control me, or over me try to rule
You told me the decisions I would make were up to me
Many lessons and heartaches in life I would learn and one day see
Mother, I remember you always tried hard to please others
Trying to keep the peace while trying to keep us all together
While still instilling in us what we could all one day be
So proud you were of all your children, Shaun, Boris, Ebony and me
You showed us the many Blessings God had given to you from above
Mother, you gave us strength, and you gave us all your love
You held me whenever I would cry out
You were always there for me whenever I was in doubt
You would sit quietly beside me and hold my hand
Listen to me, then softly say, "it will be alright, I understand"
Sometimes I felt that I had let you down
But when I hurt and I reached out to you, you were always around
I finished school, set out to get me a college degree
For I knew in life, there was more that I could be
Then, God gave to me a daughter, my life
after that was never the same
God gave to me what every woman dreams
to be, when a Mother I became
Ash'Janae I love you, you were the world to me

Marlene Wheeler Scott

"Pumpkin", you became my life and even
more of a reason to get my degree
I want to tell my family, to all come together, please be strong
Know that what happened was not because
I had done anything wrong
I do not know why I was there, at this time and at this place
But, I am sure it will be the subject of much debate
I know I have left loved ones grieving and asking God, "why"?
Saying, "we were not even given a chance to say "good-bye"
Today, as my daughter, Mother, Father, and family gathers round me
To say their good-byes for this one last time, me to see
I want all to know that I truly loved you all so, but please, do not cry
In your hearts I will always be with, so, I do not say, good-bye
Mother, watch over and take care of my daughter, "Pumpkin"
Raising her to follow her dream, not to keep
thinking of what could have been
I know from you she will always get only good advice
I know you will never leave her, and she will always be in my sight
I took your advice to never judge a person
or tell them what they must do
Until we too have walked in their shoe

Mother, I never said it often enough I know
But thank you for your love and helping me to grow
I love you Mother, so very, very much
I know I am in your heart, we will never be out of touch
Mother, I felt your love surrounding me as I laid upon that ground
You kept your promise, that you would always be around
Know too, as I closed my eyes, I heard God, my name He called out
Mother, God took me home, of this I have no doubt

God Inspired The Best in Me

I WROTE THIS POEM FOR SHIELA, THE MOTHER OF KESHIAL WHO PASSED AWAY SUDDENLY SATURDAY LEAVING BEHIND HER DAUGHTER ASH'JANAE, BROTHERS SHAUN AND BORIS AND A SISTER EBONY...... PEACE AND COMFORT TO EACH AND EVERYONE AND GOD BLESS

MOTHER

Mother, I see all your family making a fuss over you
Not just because of who you are, but for all you do
All our grandchildren and loved ones I see giving you a kiss
Saying "we love you, you are number one on our list"
You will get so emotional, I know you will
When they all show you and tell you how they feel
But, you deserve it Mother, for you are the best
To me, you stand apart, from all the rest
Mother, I want you to feel my presence with you today
If you listen closely you will also hear me say
Mother, I love you with all my heart
We will never be separated or apart
The Lord in His wisdom gave to me
A Mother who gave me happiness and so much glee
So, on this day, from my home in Heaven above
I send to you, a very special love
HAPPY MOTHER'S DAY

<u>WRITTEN FOR BETTY EVANS</u>
<u>HER FIRST MOTHER'S DAY AFTER THE PASSING OF HER SON</u>
<u>KEVIN EVANS</u>

Movin' on Up

The day has come when we will now say good-bye
Giving everyone, hugs and kisses while we all cry
Because a friend, a family loved one is moving away
All the way up, to good old PA
Of course we do not want to see them go
But since they are, we want them to know
We will miss you and we love you very much
But, you know, we will always be in touch
We know that it was for you, a hard decision to make
Becoming one among many, a great debate
But, no more decisions now, it is over and done
Positive reasons for going vs. negative to stay, won
We wish you God speed and the very best
Keep in touch by telephone, face book or by text
Your life there is a new beginning with your family to start
Your decision we know, came straight from your heart
Keep listening to your heart, you will then do what is right
Matt/Britany....you have always enjoyed a good fight
This one too you will win, obstacles you will overcome
God will tell you both, JOB WELL DONE

Matt/Britany/Tripp/Trinity/Mattie
God Bless you and keep you safe

Marlene Wheeler Scott

My Bedtime Story

I want to tell you a story about
A family, who without a doubt
Withstood many hardships and pain for each
But, they had a Mother who eased the pain and kept the peace
Being a Mother was the job she loved most
And she worked hard to keep her family close
Watching them grow and each going out on their own
Knowing all would be well, once they were grown
She too went through many a heartache
Losing two sons and a husband, her heart did break
Three sons, five daughters were now still at home
But, she made sure they would never be alone
An education she also made sure was had by all
Though a small woman, she was so proud, she was walking tall
She watched each of her children leave home and go out
Becoming their own person, and she had no doubt
That they would always remain close, in touch with each other
She had instilled in them as the teachings of a Mother
Mary, her first born, the first of the children to marry
Married a wonderful man Charlie, the future
together they would now carry
For God already knew that in the future, the role they would play
Not only opening their own home to her Mother one day
And as the oldest, she would soon start keeping together
Their own families, as well as that of their sisters and brothers
Marlene, she had struggled, but her Mother knew
She would okay as soon as her Faith in God grew

Lots, her husband Frank, their daughter and son
So unbelievable what she has overcome
Worked so hard, moving, suffering much loss
Never gave up, became owner of her own company, her own boss
Shirleen, !WOW!, so much work in her church
As she and her husband Edgar took in children who had been hurt
Michelle, the youngest of all the girls
Worked hard, grew strength from all obstacles
at her that had been hurled
But, she raised her family, kept God in her life
Overcoming so much trouble and strife
Her son Roy, the oldest boy of the lot
Went for his dream, he became a Doc
He and Pam raised a family, daughter and son
Mother was so proud of what he had done

Jerry, loving his wife Pam, their two sons,
Mother was always concerned
As he fought for his country and though they
said it was given, it was earned
A Purple Heart, for having been wounded in a war that he fought
Becoming a POW/ having been captured and caught
While fighting for our country to try and keep the peace
And Praying to God and with others that all wars would cease
Garry Lee, the youngest of all her family
Made her as proud as any Mother could be
Now that most of her other children had moved on
They became bonded, growing very close, this Mother and son
He too then joined the Army to help defend
Our peace at home, hoping too this war would soon end

Marlene Wheeler Scott

Mother's heart was aching and she was so concerned
She prayed to God for all her son's safe return
But Mother never stopped thanking God for having given to her
The strength to take on life, no matter what occurred
She taught her children to have respect
For ALL people and never to just expect
To hold out their hand and ask people for
Monies, unless they wanted paid for having done a chore
She said life will only give to you what you have put in
And Love and Faith in God, that is where it will all begin
Though our Mother, the head of the household has passed on
Her work here on earth continues, it is not done
Each of her children, with families now of their own
Will pass on her teachings, to their children,
the values of life they have known
Now, each of her children can go to be each night
Saying "Good night Mother" because of you, we are all alright

Written July 30, 2015

My Daughter

It does not seem like it was that long ago
That you were born and I watched you grow
That memorable year was 1964
When God gave to me, a baby girl, I had always prayed for
Yes, a beautiful baby girl He gifted to me
Making me the proud Mother of another child now have three
As the only girl her brothers all made sure
That she was being protected against any problems she may incur
You grew into a woman, I thought you were one of a kind
For you knew just what you wanted, was
not afraid to speak your mind
No matter what others did, or tried taking you down
You were your own person and you stood your ground
You met a man and right from the start
You knew this was the one, he had indeed won your heart
You and Rodney, got married, your dream of a family, soon came true
You became the Mother of beautiful daughters, yes, you had two
Mellisa, you have worked hard all of your life
Overcoming much sickness and lots of strife
You were a wife, a Mother, a grandmother and a friend
Even a career, you were able to blend in
Yes, in just one person this all belongs
To a special lady who is thoughtful, lovely and very strong
Who is she?...She is my world and I love her a lot
So proud of you My Daughter, MELLISA LYNN SCOTT

Marlene Wheeler Scott

My Last Wish

Lord, before you take me home, Please
There is one last thing that I want to ask of Thee
Because, before I take my last breath
To go with you into Eternal Rest
I want all of my children, all of my family
To be gathered round me, my last time to see
I want them to know that I am not saying to them, "good-bye"
But, I would be leaving, to go to my Heavenly Home in the sky
Where I will also be waiting for that final Trumpet Call
When God gathers his faithful, one and all
I want to tell my family to be strong, and not weak
When some urges, or other pleasures you may seek
Do not indulge in parties or wild nights out
For that is not what happiness is all about
I want to tell them to not wait until they grow old
Then look back, regretting what you have left in the fold
Remember, it is God who you should be reaching
And to remain to His teaching
Trust in God, the morals that I have instilled in you
That remained with you as into adulthood you grew
Now, into your own families you can instill
These morals, it is called DOING GOD'S WILL
You must trust in God no matter what
Forever thanking him for all the blessings you have got
Asking God to guide you and to forgive you of your sins
So we can all be together in Heaven again
Today, I go to rest and as I now close my eyes
Remember, I love you, we will again meet, this is not GOOD-BYE

God Inspired The Best in Me

My Open Prayer to God

Heavenly Father, I know that You can see
What is happening to our Church and our Ministry
There is so much turmoil that is beginning to exist within
Arguments of where we are going and where we have been
Many of our members who have walked through our Church door
Are now leaving because they say this is
not what they were looking for
Yes, in the beginning, they put in their money and their time
But Greed took over and each proclaimed that, "this church is mine"
But God, I know that NO ONE owns you
And God, You are the Church, is this not true?
'The body of the church, we come, we
worship, work hard, do all we can
To do Thy Will and Your promise of one
day, going to the Promised Land
Our Pastor, Your Chosen, Your word and
from his heart he will preach
While reaching out to All that he can reach
It is true that monies are needed for the church overhead
But, in an open field, your sheep can also be fed
There is no need to spend monies to have a Splendid looking church
But spend the monies on the homeless and those that hurt
We say we are doing God's Will and reaching out
That is what God says spreading His word, that is what it is all about
Not the number of people who will show up in church each day
If not your quota, closing your doors and turning God's people away
God says we are not to close our church doors, even if there is just one

Marlene Wheeler Scott

That may be the young heart whose heart God had just won
We should all be standing together, stand our ground and be strong
Raising our voices to God in praises and in song
I truly believe that we are being tested, our church and all
But the faithful will stay and our church will not fall
So God, my prayer to you is that we do Your Will so that all will see
We are reaching out to all, here at LAKESIDE
OUTREACH MINISTRIES

My Remembrance of Ms. Jane

From this lady, so many blessing I received
Now, today, I stand here and I grieve
I grieve because we will no longer be able to see
This beautiful lady who meant so much to others and to me
Her love for her family and life, there could never be a denial
Because no matter her pain, for others she always had a smile
I first met Ms. Jane about six years ago
She made an impression on me that continued to grow
Because of her health, she was wheelchair bound
But, her family and friends made sure she always got around
She loved coming down to the Lake
And when she did, make no mistake
I would go visit with her and hold her hand
She had a love for life that we all need to understand
There were times when I became depressed or was in pain
All I needed to do, was think of Ms. Jane
She went through so much, only she could know
But, always a smile, she tried never to let her pain show
Her grandchildren, she simply loved and adored
She could only watch them play, hold them,
always wishing she could do more
Her daughter Becky and her husband
Thomas, were always by her side
Their hurting for her they hid, but their love for her they did not hide
Her companion, friend, caretaker Peggy, who for so many years
There when ever needed, I know she too is grieving and in tears
I too stand here, I see you and yes, I too will cry

Marlene Wheeler Scott

But, I am not going to say "good-bye"
For I know Ms. Jane, that you are now at peace
All your pain and suffering have now ceased
Your love and memories will continue to surround us everywhere
Those memories with everyone will continue to be shared
I know today, to Heaven with God you did ascend
Ms. Jane, I love you and I will miss you, my forever friend

In Loving Memory
Oct 15th, 2015

My Son Steven
April 06, 1967

Fourty-eight years ago, God gave to me
Another special son, Steven, he was son number three
He has been special in so many, many ways
With him, we never had a dull day
He was so energetic, so full of fun
But, did not like school, he often tried to shun
But, some things need learned and not just guessin'
From his school of Hard Knocks, I think he learned his lesson
He is a young man now, he has really grown
Married, has a son now of his own
He loves his only son, there is no doubt
He will advise him well on the ins and outs
We are very proud of him and what he has done
Our son Steven, our number three Son

My Stairway to Heaven

The day I was born, it began my first step
Then every step of my life thereafter, I truly felt
Because the imprints of my steps that I was leaving behind
Would become the story of the life that was to be mine
Throughout the years these steps grew and grew
God had His reason, at the time, I never knew
I only knew that every step I took was leading me somewhere
Sometimes they became heavy, but, they were my steps to bear
In prayer to God I asked Him about the
reason for these footsteps of mine
He said, "you are building your ladder to Heaven, one step at a time"
So, I will keep walking, leaving one step at a time
Leaving my imprints of my Legacy behind
Then, when I have taken my last step
And I hear God say, "My word to you I have kept"
Your ladder to the Stairway to Heaven has now been let down
Know that each step you take now, leads to
Heaven...You will be HEAVEN BOUND

NEWSMEN & REPORTERS

Shame on you if you try to overlook
All these white collar crooks
As Americans, we trust you and we believe
In what we hear from you and what we see
So, if we hear that all is going well
But suddenly, we see our country is going to "Hell"
Then we begin doubting what we are being told
Our Government is not Transparent, but part of a Mold
A mold that keeps growing, taking in everything in sight
Until we finally begin to see the light
We then begin to say, "enough is enough"
Demanding to clean house, removing all the "old stuff"
So, all you reporters, both on or off the air
Reporting the New is supposed to Balanced and Fair
You should not try to degrade or put down
The few honest newsrooms and reporters around
A FOX is sly, he will stalk his Prey
Keeping them in sight, not letting them get away
When they are caught, they know they are in trouble
The game is over and the Truth will burst their bubble
Fox News cannot be bought
For FAIR and BALANCED NEWS they have fought
If it is for our country an d the people that you care
You too will report the truth, if you so dare
You are the reporters upon whose news we must rely
Being transparent, telling the truth and above all, not lie
Even if it is something in which you may not agree

Marlene Wheeler Scott

You need to be fair and balanced, by reporting both sides to see
If someone in our Government is being corrupt
Shame on you if you try to cover it up
And shame on you and the other stations
For not being honest to us about problems facing our nation
So, if you know something or someone is off base
Verify the facts first, do not write them in haste
Then report the facts, but, time, you should not waste
There should be never a doubt
To report and bring this person out
Because in case you have forgot
You are accountable to we the people, and trust and belief means a lot

Nikki

Nikki...I know that you cannot wait
And I know that you will not hesitate
To go out on this, your very special date
With family and friends, who will help you celebrate
This day is special for you because it comes but once a year
But, it is a day that we all look forward to and hold so dear
For you, on this date you began your life on earth
When God chose your parents, and your Mother to you gave birth
They watched you grow, they were always there
Letting you know they loved you and they really cared
Now, on this, your Special God given day
Your family and friends have all gathered here to say
"We love you Nikki, you know that we do
We are here, not only today, but always here for you
Nikki, you were/are, a wonderful Mother and a wife
God blessed you with this 'special gift', He called it 'life'
Yes, it is a special gift for a special person, and we all want to say
Nikki, we love you and wish you a very !!!!HAPPY BIRTHDAY

03/29/2015
<u>MAY GOD GRANT YOU THAT WISH THAT YOU ARE LOOKING FOR</u>

No Big Deal

Sometimes the pressures that I feel
Pressures that sometimes, I say, "it's no big deal"
One pressure I feel is that I am so alone
That I have no friends, no place to go, I am on my own
I know it is true, others have problems, some worse than mine
Somehow, they have learned to deal with them in time
They are able to go on with their life
Handling their problems and their strife
But, maybe they had that very special someone
who stood by them, encouraged them that they could overcome
Well, I thought that I too had a friend
That when in need, upon them I could call and depend
But when I called out to them, no one was there
I felt so alone, I felt that no one cared
One day when I cried out, I heard a voice
Saying, "my child, it is you who must make the choice
For it is upon yourself that you must learn to depend
You will find in yourself, there is no better friend
But you must still love Thy neighbor, be kind to them all
Letting them know you are there, if and when they should call"
God also told me, that beside me, He would always be there
Because He loved me and He cared
He said that I would soon find an answer
to my problem, then I would feel
That compared to others, my problem was NO BIG DEAL

God Inspired The Best in Me

Our Family Reunion {Scott}
June 27th, 2015

I have thought long and bard about this day
Trying to find the right words to say
To all of my family that will be gathering here
My family, that I love so much and hold so dear
This is the day that I have long awaited for
My wish now, is that there will be many more
Here today, Mike, my oldest son, my first born
MY son Mark, in spirit, so loved, of him we still mourn
Mellisa, my only daughter, I am so proud of her
Steven, my last son of him, I love them all, that's for sure
Grandchildren, nine of them, we have been truly blessed
Whew! Somebody needs to take a rest
Johnny, Brittany, Ashley, Royce, Crystle, Keri
Steven Jr./ Tressa and Tori
In each of them lies lots of memories and lots of stories
But one thing for sure, of all of them l am so proud
God blessed me with all that Heaven would allow
Then, Great Grandchildren I too have been given
Assuring that our generations will keep on livin'
K.J./Braylon/Maddox/Brianna/Blake/Alonica/Kahleina/and Cayden
I am told that there is another one, soon awaitin'
There are some others that I want to mention too
I have not forgotten about any of you
Some of you have married into and became part of our family

Marlene Wheeler Scott

But without you, our families would not be Philip/Victor/
Brandon/Rodney/Jeffrey/Jason/Denia/Chris/Patti/Johnny/Paul
Some are son-in-laws, daughter-in-laws
Some are our special adopted family, we love you all
Again, I want to say to all of you
"Thank you" for being you and all that you do
You all have families, jobs, going to school every day
Some live long distances, I know it is hard to get away
But, I do not think of us as being a part
For you are forever with me and in my heart
We will leave here today a little closer to each other
All because we have taken the time to come together
"Thank you again" is all that I can say
Except, we love you and we will always remember this day

OVIEDA ROSE
Feb. 06th, 1935-Jan.19th, 2014

God tell us that even our Souls too have a Season
And for everything that happens, there is a reason
Why am I so cast down and so despondently sad?
When all I long for is to be happy and glad
Why does my heart feel so heavy with so much weight?
All I want to do is escape from this soul-saddened state
I quietly ask God and myself why life has to be this way
Why has my happiness been silenced in a heart that was so gay?
But then God showed me and suddenly it all became so clear
That the Soul too has a Season just like the year
He said that I too must pass through life's Autumn of dying
Which is a desolate time of heartbreak, hurt, and crying
Then it is followed by Winter holding in it's frostbitten hand
A heart that has become as frozen as all the snow covered land
Yes, I now know I too must pass through
all the seasons that God sends
I am now content in knowing that one day everything ends
But what a Blessing it is to know that God has His reasons
And for us to find our Soul, we too must have our seasons
We get strength in knowing that after the Autumn time sadness
It will soon be filled by a Springtime filled with gladness
Yes, God says that He chooses only the best
And today we see one of them being laid to rest
A wonderful, beautiful woman whom God has chose
Our loving Mother, Ovieda Rose

Feb. 06th, 1935-Jan. 19th, 2014

Marlene Wheeler Scott

PAM & PAULA

We all know, and we are all aware
That one day, sometime, somewhere
In our life time, we will lose
A loved one, one that only God will chose
As parents, we all want to see our children grow
And pray to God to let us be the first to go
Because we do not want our children to see our pain
In life, from them, we try so hard to sub stain,
The fact that we are aging, now just praying for a tomorrow
Not wanting our children or loved ones to see our sorrow
But, we know these sufferings at sometime, we all must bear
I do not want my suffering with my children, they have to share
I want you to know, though my mind and body are growing weak
And words I am unable to speak
God showed me and He made me aware
That you were beside me and that you cared
I also seen you, though you did not know
You were talking of memories and looking at old photos
I love you both, you have stayed beside me for so long
Paula even sang to me, some of her songs
God kept me here like this for a reason you see
And if I could speak I would tell you what I believe
It made all of you stronger and brought you together
Made you love and respect one another
God knows what He is doing, it is not for us to ask Why?
We simply thank God and said, "YES, GOD, I WILL TRY"

God Inspired The Best in Me

Phyllis....Forever Remembered
Feb. 1946---Aug. 2015

God says that although He has taken her home
He says that she did not leave her loved ones alone
She told God she was ready and felt that she was prepared
As she had left loved ones in each others care
She said she knew that they would take care of each other
And would continue to carry on, the teachings of their Mother
Phyllis was so proud of all her family
Was so happy for the time that God had given her to see
Her dreams come true, her children grow into adulthood
Knowing with God's help, she did the best that she could
A loving husband, together were they for so many years
Facing life, sharing their dreams and sharing their tears
A dream for children, Adam, Erin, Kyle, they had three
Their dream came true, they were now a complete family
So, Phyllis, rest in peace and know that your teachings
Are still being carried on and they are now reaching
Out to all your future generations
Phyllis, everyone will continue to feel your vibrations
Know that we will continue to forever feel your touch
Know also that we love you very much
Phyllis, you were a wife, a Mother, a forever friend
Your memory will live with us forever, it will never end.

Marlene Wheeler Scott

PRAYING-NO SET TIME

I used to set aside a time every day
When I would take the time to pray
I waited anxiously for that time to draw near
Vowing to let nothing or no one interfere
For it was that very special time
I could quietly sit with God and tell Him what was on my mind
But, one day when I began to pray
I heard a voice gently but quietly say,
"Why do you set just one special time aside for me,
For I am here with you always, whatever the need
Yes, I want you to have that quiet time
To spend with Me, telling me what is on your mind,
But the time you set aside should not always be
The only time that you talk to me
Prayers must be genuine and from the heart
From this I want you never to depart
Know that I am here, I am always around
Whenever you need Me, just call out, God, I need you now
If you need me, you know through prayer I can be found
You do not have to wait for Prayer Time to roll around"
To talk to me about whatever you need
Just take My hand, I will lead

God Inspired The Best in Me

Ranting and Raving

Should I rant or should I rave
About all these feelings that I have saved
I really do let some things get to me
Why can't some people just let me be?
I know that I am not perfect, but then no one is
No excuses, but we all have at one time gone amiss
If you do not like the way that I dress
Or the way that I live, then I must confess
These are my choices, made only by me
So, don't judge me based only on what you see
I work hard for a living, I have lots of friends
Who knows I am here and on me they can depend
I do not talk or go behind their back
I think people who do, are really slack
If I am married and together, we have a problem
Then we handle it together, just me and him
If I should be in need of financial help, at some time, we all do
I will find a way, there are trusted friends I can turn to
If I am sick and I am in need of prayer
I want the prayers from those who are sincere and really care
I really think that it all boils down
To some disgruntled people who have not found
Their own true self or how to be happy
So, they try to heap onto others, their own misery
As for myself, I am doing fine
Call me if you want, that I must be one of a kind

But my God says that we are ALL as one
It is He who has the final say when all is done
So, there you have it, what more can I say?
Except, God Bless you and you have a great day

Remembering Sammy Bryant
10/2014

I did not know this young man
But, I do know it is very hard to understand
How we can be with someone one minute
Then suddenly, no longer in our lives, they are in it
I understand that he was a "forever friend"
Who showed his love to alright up to the end
Only God has the answers to the questions we ask
And only He can give us peace, for loved ones passed
I also heard he loved to draw, an artist I heard them say
So, maybe if we all look up into the sky one day
We will see beautiful colors making the Heaven's glow
It will be Sammy drawing us another colorful rainbow
Sammy, to all your friends and your family too
God's peace and understanding, as they say "good-bye" to you
But, know that you will be remembered forever here
For you were loved, you were very special, that is clear
You left your mark on all around
Before you became Heaven bound

Marlene Wheeler Scott

REUNION
OUR FAMILY GATHERING

Well, here it is, another whole year
We give thanks to God, to all who could be here
Loved ones who have gathered from all around
Those who live close and those from out of town
Yes, this is our chosen time when we come together
Being able to hug and talk, not just by phone or by a letter
Time for catching up on all the news, both new and old
Listening to stories that our ancestors before us told
Our now older generation looking upon the young
Proud of how far, each generation has come
For now, each generation will carry on where the other left off
Carrying on a tradition that we hope will never stop
So, as we gather again this year, united as one
We will eat, enjoy being together, and have lots of fun
Then, God willing, we will meet again, same time next year
To again hold and embrace those that we hold so dear
God Bless and God speed, be safe returning to your home
Till we meet again, let's keep in touch by letter or by phone

WRITTEN FOR MY SISTER IN CHRIST, MY FRIEND, POLLY McLEOD
FOR HER FAMILY REUNION SATURDAY, MAY 4TH, 2013
THANK YOU POLLY FOR LETTING ME BE A PART

Right Foot or Wrong Foot

Have you ever done something while in a rush?
Making everything you do, go wrong, no matter what you touch?
Well, it happened to me one morning when I got up
What was in store for me was about to develop
This morning I got up, got dressed, then put on my shoes
Started getting ready for work as I always do
But, somehow' this morning, something did not seem right
For one, the shoes I put on my feet seemed to be very tight
A few minutes later it dawned on me
What I did, I looked down and said, "how stupid could I be?"
All because I made myself try to hurry, not taking my time
Because I thought I was going to be late, I was running behind
He put in my way this morning what I called a roadblock
Which made me slow down and of myself take stock
'Slow down' was the message that to be was being sent
And when I did, I suddenly knew what God had meant
He let me know that sometimes we get so
involved in our own little world
We fail to see others or their problems that around them swirl
We can ALL sometimes get off on the wrong foot
Simply by saying the wrong word, that is all that it took
Then, those things we said we would try to overlook or avert
Not realizing that these words had caused hurt
The hurt and the pain from words that are so unkind
Could have all been avoided if we had only taken the time
Starting the day off on the wrong foot is not the way
That I choose or want to start my day

Marlene Wheeler Scott

I thank you God for having let me see
What my day could have been, but now, how it will be
A day so wonderful, not filled with a lot of strife
God, thank you for being a part of my life
Well, I went to work, yes, I was even on time
Walking in with a smile and a big "HELLO",
I greeted the co-workers of mine
They in turn all smiled and said to me, "well hello"
Now this is the way every day should go
When I get up now to start my day anew
I will take the time to 'put on the right shoe'
To all of my family, loved ones and friends I want to say
It is we that can make sure we all have a great day
I found if we put our shoe on the wrong
foot and try to walk…it will hurt
So it is with words spoken out of haste, that we sometimes 'blurt'

Let us not get off on the wrong foot with each other
But be mindful and considerate and work together
Let us not judge someone for something until
We walk in their shoes and know how they fill
Like a good shoe, a good friendship will not wear out
Being there for each other, no matter if it is through rain or drought

Remember: A shoe can last a long time if it has a GOOD SOLE

Rodney/Mellisa
Our Love

Two people who fall in love, never to part
This is what makes for a perfect heart
A heart that becomes a symbol of a love so true
Vows of togetherness, between the both of you
Today, as you look back and remember those vows
You smile, saying, we made it this far, but how?
You both have had your ups and downs
You both have stood on some shakey grounds
But, you know you made it because of your love for each other
Your vow to honor, love and to always remain togetherness
There is nothing that cannot be overcome when we understand
Each other, our wants, our needs and hold each others hand
So, on this day, Our Special Day, I want so much to say
I still love you, but even more than I did yesterday
Being with each other is our symbol of our love
Til one day, God takes us both to Heaven above

Written for my daughter Mellisa and her husband Rodney, their Anniversary

SHARING and REMEMBERING

BETTY, I said a Prayer for you today
ASKING God to send peace and comfort your way
I know it has been almost a year
Since you lost a loved one so dear
In such a short time, you've lost your husband and your son
A terrible loss to bear for anyone
I know if we could have one wish at our command
We would change what happened with the wave of a hand
But, you know that Kevin is gone, that is a, finality
But, he remains alive in memory, that is a reality
I know your heart is heavy, but it has been your strong belief
In God, and your faith in Him, that has eased your grief
I too lost a son, it was so suddenly
I felt my whole world had come crashing down upon me
I prayed to God to give me the words to say
To a friend who was remembering her son today
Betty my friend, I share your hurt and your pain
But, God promised us Sunshine, after the Rain
God said "death is not and ending
But an Afterlife, the start of a new beginning"
Kevin made an impact on all those that he met
Leaving you with wonderful memories, you will never forget
I feel Kevin would say to you, "one day we will be together
But until that day, remember, I LOVE YOU MOTHER"

Written for my good friend, Betty Evans whose son was taken so quickly

God Inspired The Best in Me

Should I Worry??

I had never worried about getting sick
I never had to wonder about what Dr. to pick
I did however worry about the cost
If for some reason my insurance I lost
But, I was always assured that they would pay
If I should find myself in a hospital one day
Then suddenly, my Government said to me
You must now change your insurance company
Prior conditions right now some Doctors will not touch
But this new plan will and you will pay half as much
Well, I changed my plan, I did what they said
But the increase from Obama Care has put me in the red
You can keep your Dr. and present insurance I was told
This was repeated so often, it soon became old
Nothing they said was true, they lied to me
They say now I have to pay, so that others can get it free
So now, if I get sick and cannot afford to pay
For the medical treatment I may need right away
The only way now is under the Obama Care
But that is only if I will pay "my fair share"
Obama thought his fix was the ultimate cure
But for many, this one thing we all know for sure
We do not need big brother to help us pick and choose
Saying, taking it now or you will lose
If I choose Obama Care, for me it would be a loss
Financially I could not afford the cost
It was a hard pill to swallow, this Obama Care Pill

Marlene Wheeler Scott

It was shoved down our throats making many of us ill
My Doctor used to say take an aspirin, go home, get some rest
Call me in the morning and we will run some tests
Now, they say, go somewhere else, I do not care where
But, wherever you go, you better have Obama Care

Speaking from the Heart

I do not know just where to start
So I guess I will just speak from the heart
I have the right to speak out too
About the things you are trying to do
I know that you will agree with me
That you also enjoy your right of being free
No one can come to your house at night
And tell you that you no longer have any rights
That you must now work for your Government
But you won't get paid, not one red cent
That we will now make millions for those who rule
And we have no voice in what we must do
Well, you are not doing what we elected you to be
You are creating a world that is your fantasy
Brave men and women have died for both me and you
So that all our dreams would one day come true
We know our country has both good and bad within
But we do not fantasize, or look the other way and pretend
We know that there is a lot of pain and sorrow
That comes with preserving our peace for tomorrow
To those who protest against our freedom, I am ashamed
When you protest against our country, do not do it in my name
Mr. President, you were our nominee
Chosen to lead us, guide us, and keep us free
We are called ONE NATION, and we are UNITED
This is not something that just one person decided
It is you who is allowing others to put our country to shame

Marlene Wheeler Scott

And we no longer want to hear that someone else is to blame
It was you we trusted, we made you are choice
But we will not let you forget that America still has a voice
We are Americans, we are proud and we stand tall
United we will stand, we will not be divided and fall

Spreading God's Word

We all look forward to that marital bliss
Between a handsome young man and a lovely young miss
Someone who together enjoys life, just for itself
Taking each day as it develops
Then, together they will ride off into the
Sunset, taking in God's Beauty
While full-filling all of their God given duties
Together they would spread God's Word along the way
Meeting with friends and strangers and together they would pray
Pray for the homeless, the sick and all those in need
While also showing others how in life they too can succeed
That though many trials they too had been through
But, they stood together and did what God told them to do
Yes, he admits to many of their past mistakes
But in finding God, a new beginning they began to make
So now they travel all over the country side
To let others know that they are losing and being denied
By using drugs or alcohol, or by any other means
When it is upon God and not on drugs or falsehoods they lean
Thank you, you are both one of a kind
Not afraid to speak out or say what is on your mind
A terrible accident they were in about a year ago
Would they make it?, we did not know
But God knew and upon them He laid His Hands
Healing them so that again, they could travel over the lands
You both have showed us all, even given us hints
That it is from God that you get your strength

Marlene Wheeler Scott

Yes, hunting and fishing, be truly loved this sport
Never came home empty handed, I am happy to report
This dynamo duo has won all our hearts
So much so that I do not know where to start
Well, I too have given you a hint, so, do you now know
Who this wonderful duo is that we respect and love so?
Well, they are truly outstanding, they are one in a ZILLION
Yes, I am speaking of MARK and DEBBIE WILLIAMS

SPRING

Yes, Spring is here, it has sprung
With it, new life has now begun
Not just for the blooming of the trees and the flowers
But another new beginning of life...ours
This is the time to talk about the birds and the bees
For love is blooming all around, feeling the gentle breeze
We all have in common, roots from which we carne
We each have days filled with Sunshine and Rain
Yes, they say with April, come the April Showers
But with it comes the blooming of many plants and flowers
Just as God douses and feeds His plants
He helps us to grow too, showing us our cans and can'ts
It all starts with the seeds He gives to us to sow
Just like the seeds, without nourishment we too cannot grow
All His beauty He gives to us and wants us too, to share
With everybody and everything, every place and every where
So, when we all SPRING into action
A new freshness of life...we will all get so much satisfaction

Marlene Wheeler Scott

Suicide-No Way to Die

I have walked alone for so long
My heart is breaking, I am trying to be strong
Strong for my children. they are my life
So, why do I feel so unworthy and full of strife?
For God, I do love my children so
All I ever wanted was to watch them grow
I feel I must be doing something wrong
I admit, I am weak, I am not strong
I have cried so many lonely tears
Wanting someone to help me, calm my fears
But when I cried out, no one was there
My pain seems more than I can bear
I have cried for someone to hear my plea
I need someone to rescue and comfort me
The hurt and pain that I feel inside
I feel will go away, the day I die
My heart is heavy, but God I do believe
That You have a plan for me
So why God, oh please tell me why
Have you not seen my pain, heard my cry?
God, if You will just show me the way
And help guide me through each day
I will do whatever you want me to
Because God, I love my children and I believe in You
My child I have seen your pain, I heard your cry
I have even heard your thoughts of Suicide
But know this, the pain that you will leave behind

Will live forever in your children and loved ones mind
Know too, it is I who will choose the time for you to go
When it is that time, you will know
You must have Faith and be not afraid
For you, your path I have already laid
Know that I never put on you more than you can bear
Hold MY Hand, I will guide you, I will always be there

Marlene Wheeler Scott

SUMMER

Summertime is here, and it has shone
It is a time for gatherings, no time to be alone
For it brings smiles and love and lots of sunshine
That comes with the warmth of Summer time
We all need sunshine and to feel it's warm embrace
That we all feel from the Sun's warm and smiling face
It is God sending us His assurance with His gentle touch
That He is always there to watch over and comfort us
The flowers too will be blooming and the birds will sing
We see God in everything the Summer time will bring
We can smell the flowers, go to the beach, have a picnic and play
God wants us all to enjoy and savor these warm Summer days
This is the time of year also for both school and other vacations
Let us get going without any hesitations
Let us take advantage of all this season imposes
Wake up each day smiling and 'smelling the roses'

TJ
Thanking Jesus

"You have Cancer", these words the Dr. said to me
But, I heard God say, "you are Cancer free"
There are tests the Doctors will have to run on you
Before they decide what they must do
The Doctor said, "in reviewing your tests"
We found Cancer in one of your breasts
Though it is showing that the Cancer is small
To be safe, surgery is needed to remove the Nipple, breast and all
I prayed to God and I put it all in His Hands
Knowing whatever happened, it was all part of His plans
God spoke to me before the surgery had begun
Saying, "my child, because of your faith,
this battle you have already won
The surgery went well, I thought it was done
But, another test, the Doctor said be now must nm
When that test came back, the Doctor shook his head and said to me
"No more tests are needed, you are 'Cancer' free
But these were words from God I had already heard
Because I kept my Faith and I believed in God's word
Thank you God, I have always had the Faith
Your are always on time, You are never late

Marlene Wheeler Scott

Taking the Time

In church this morning, I was looking around
For a faithful church member, she could not be found
She has never missed a Sunday, she is always there
Because she loves her God and for others she cares
I thought I would just sit and wait
Thinking maybe she was running a little late
But when the service was over and she still had not showed
I knew something was wrong and where I had to go
When I got to her home, no answer I got
All her doors and windows were locked
I started to knock on the door once again
When suddenly, I heard crying from within
I called for help, then I kicked in the door
There inside, lying on the floor
My friend, saying for two days she had laid there
She thought no one was coming because no one cared
She said that morning when to God she again prayed
God said, "you will be alright, someone is on the way"
God, when I saw my friend I was overcome with delight
Thank You God, I know everything is going to be alright
God for me, You showed me that no matter what or how busy we get
We need to take the time for each other, we must never forget

Teresa

I know you did not think that you would get by
On this, your special day, without me saying "HI"
For you, this year has been hard but also Blessed
Things happened to you that you would never have guessed
Your heartache over dissention from a beloved daughter
Your prayer for her now is that she follows
God and what has been taught her
You are still mourning for the man who was your backbone
Still hurting from the death of your Father,
feeling like you are all alone
But Teresa, God sent another man He knew would be by your side
So devoted and a love he had for you could not be denied
Teresa, it is your Faith in God that has brought you through
Because with every obstacle, God has been there for you
Your earthly Father and your Heavenly Father are both looking down
Saying, "We love you Teresa, smile, do not frown"
You r earthly Father, Rev. Tidwell, taught
you that God would always be
The one to talk to, He would ease your mind and set you free
God gave you a gift He wanted you to share with others
Your love of music, singing, praising God, bringing so many together
It is true, we know not what tomorrow may bring
But today, we can lift our voices to God, His praises we will sing
God does not on us keep a file, instead, He
listens to and hears our Prayers
Teresa, God created you and you know that He cares
This is the day that God has given to you

Marlene Wheeler Scott

He watched you grow, doing the things you were born to do
So, gather with all your friends and your beloved family
Enjoying this day, God wants you to be happy
Your father Leo I know will also be there
Because he too loved you and he really cared
He is proud that you have kept his Legacy alive
His Ministry and new generations, because of you will survive
Teresa, from me and all your friends and family we want to say
!!!!TERESA CLINE, HAPPY, HAPPY BIRTHDAY"

The Day I Left

Today I fought back the tears of seeing someone I loved
Being laid to rest, but I knew he was going to be in Heaven above
I listened to the words being said about him that day
And yes, the tears flowed and I too began to pray
A peace then came over me, I do not know why
But, I felt God beside me, I felt at peace and could no longer cry
I then hugged everyone, I told them I loved them and I cared
Mother, you and I, a great big hug and kiss we both shared
My life has not been perfect, I've done things of which I am not proud
But, I heard God say, "I had given you all that Heaven would allow"
God also knew that I was not good at saying good-bye
And I truly feel that this is why
He chose that day to quickly and quietly step in
Because I found peace with God, I felt He had forgiven me of my sin
To my Mother, I know you will always carry me in your heart
No good-byes because we will never be apart
To all my children, grandchildren, and Irene, my wife
You were my love, the reason for my life
To my brothers, we remained close, always had a ball
Getting together, laughing and enjoying
the memories we would recall
Remember me, and remember I did not say good-bye
Because we will all be together again, one day in Heaven on High

KEVIN EVANS
KILLED SUDDENLY THE SAME DAY HE HELPED LAY TO REST HIS COUSIN
EARL MILES

Marlene Wheeler Scott

The Revolving Door

As I was sitting and watching this revolving door
I found myself thinking more and more
Of people and things who had entered my life but did not stay
Going out the Revolving Door, whose doors went both ways

The Revolving Door stayed busy, just like in my life
So busy, with so many things and much strife
I have not been perfect, I am the first to admit
But, my life did not come with a map or prepared skit

I recalled one day when I had felt low and in much despair
I kept looking for help, for someone who would care
I remember looking up toward the Heavens and crying out
"Lord help me, please take away my fears and my doubts

God told me that He was opening the door for me
As it revolves around, the more that I would see
That us we try to exit, we always leave something behind
But even on the other side of door, there is an exit sign

New things He said I would encounter there
I would meet new people who, yes, they would care
So, as I watched that door open, then go round and round
When I go through it, I would be Heaven Bound

God Inspired The Best in Me

T-H-E
Take Heed Everyone

THE most powerful force in life is Love
THE greatest asset in Faith
THE most powerful channel of communication is Prayer
THE most important thing in life is The Power of God
THE greatest joy is Giving
THE worst thing to be without is Hope
THE most destructive habit is Worry
THE greatest loss is the Loss of Self Respect
THE ugliest personality trait is Selfishness
THE greatest problem to overcome is Fear
THE most beautiful attire to wear is A Smile
THE most crippling disease is Excuses
THE most dangerous pariah is Gossip
THE most powerful words are I Can
THE most effective sleeping pill is Peace of Mind
THE greatest shot in the arm is Encouragement
THE most prized possession is Integrity
THE most satisfying work is Helping Others
THE greatest attitude is called Gratitude

GRATITUDE unfolds the Goodness of Life

Marlene Wheeler Scott

To All My Grandchildren

One of the happiest times upon this earth
Is when children, God gives to us to birth
To then love them, protect them, watch them grow
Teach them right from wrong, so one day they will know
That when they too grow into adulthood
They have taught their children the way they should
When I see my children grow and leave the 'nest'
I wipe away my tears and pray I have done my best
I will watch as they too grow and begin to have their own families
Soon, I will have grandchildren they will be sharing with me
Then, I will watch them running around the yard having fun
The same thing that their parents, my children had done
God is good and I am so thankful for
All the grands and great grands and I hear still more
I know that one day I will be leaving this earth
Knowing that this generation will keep growing with each new birth
Six granddaughters, three grandsons
Six great-grandsons and 3 great granddaughters, the girls got outdone
But one more is now on the way
Tie breaker, boy or girl? Healthy is what I pray
Nine girls and nine boys, thank you Lord
For a family that I love and adore

God Inspired The Best in Me

<u>Grandchildren;</u>
<u>Johnny..,Royce...Steven</u>
<u>Crystle...Keri...Tressa...Tori...Brittnay....Ashley</u>

<u>Great Grandchildren:</u>
<u>Brianna...Alonica....Kahleina....Blake...Braylon...Kyle Jr.{ K.J.}</u>
<u>Cayden...Maddox....Grayson.....{?}{one on the way, Brittany}</u>

To My Family

Sometimes we get so caught up in our own tears and pain
That we only count ours losses and not our gains
Today, I fought back the tears of seeing someone I loved
Being laid to rest, being taken to Heaven above
Suddenly I felt a peace come over me
I felt God was standing dose, and I felt free
I felt God had forgiven me also of my sins
And then He quickly and quietly stepped in
Mother, you were my world, to me you meant so much
Always there when needed with a Mother's tender touch
Only you were able to put up with someone like me
Maybe because I was your youngest, your loving son of three
To my brothers and friends, I ask you all to stay strong
Keep your faith in God even when things seem to go wrong
To my wife, I loved you and now it is up to you
To stay strong for our children and grandchildren, they need you too
Bonita, my cousin and also my dear friend
Please know that you did not cause my life to end
No one knows when or why or even who God will choose
He does not send ahead, sending out little clues
For when it is our time to go
Sometimes, like me, it will be quick, one never knows
You had just come from seeing your only brother laid to rest
When God laid upon you another test
Know God at times will at times place upon us pain and sorrow
Not to punish us but to make us stronger for tomorrow
I believe that God has placed a test upon all of my family

God Inspired The Best in Me

You all need to now come together in love,
living in peace and harmony
So, I leave this, with all of you this, my one last Prayer
Until we all meet again one day with the Man upstairs

KEVIN EVANS
A MOTORCYCLE ACCIDENT/SAME DAY AS HIS COUSIN'S FUNERAL

TRIPP

God, do not let this illness get a 'grip'
On this young child, we call Tripp
Heal his body, God we pray
And take all his pain away
Please look down upon this child
He is so young, a child so meek and mild
So many hearts he has won
Even though he is only one{1}
But he is so wise for his young years
He has brought much joy to all his 'piers'
He comes to church on Sunday with his grandpa, J.C.
The bond of love between these two is plain to see
He brings joy to us all in so many ways
Seeing him lift his hands to God in praise
Yes, he brings a smile to all of us
This child, so many hearts he has touched
He is very blessed, yes indeed
One day, this child Tripp will lead

It was Nov. 24, 2003, Tripp was in the hospital very, very sick and he was in much prayer...Today, this young man is doing well, in school and has two beautiful sisters

God Inspired The Best in Me 249

VOICES

Well here it is, Monday night
And I just decided I would write
About the things that are coming to my mind
It does not matter if the words do not rhyme
It seems as though every time I hear a voice
I start to do it, I hear another saying, you have a choice
When someone says something that confuses me
Another voice says, "not all is as it seems to be
I sometimes wonder why things are happening, the way they are
Then I hear a voice saying, "you have come so far
Do not let others take you down
When at last, Jesus you have found"
I think about my life a year ago
And how I felt my life had become so low
That there was no need for me to live, I had no one
Then I heard a voice saying, "I gave to you my Son"
Though at times, things still give me grief and pain
This voice keeps telling me to just look at what I have gained
I still do not understand fully what is happening to me
But I will keep doing whatever it is that God wants me to be
So, if you look for me, I can be found
Standing here on this higher ground
Just waiting to hear the voice of Jesus say
"Keep your feet planted, for I will be back one day"
The grounds are high and solid, not soft like clay
My feet are firmly planted, I will not stray
For I now know that Satan no longer has me bound
Since God lifted me and placed me on a Higher Ground

We Were Meant to Be

I know that God put us both in this place
Where first we met, and we saw each others face
We knew right then and there
We were meant to be together, we both
had looked for love, everywhere

Yes, I used to dream of what I called, "the perfect man"
One that would someday reach out and take my hand
He would make my heart begin to skip a beat
And would sweep me right off my feet

Today, I told you I would become your wife
With you, together we will begin our new life
I feel that there is nothing that will ever compare
To the love and the joy that we both now share

Then, when that wonderful day is over and done
God having joined us together, uniting us as one
We will live our lives together throughout all eternity
Thank you God for sending him to me

Beanard & Brittany...He proposed Christmas Day and she said yes
God Bless you both

God Inspired The Best in Me

Welcome Home My Child

Today begins a new life for me
For God has lifted me and set me free
Yes, God gave me life, many years ago
Then He watched over me as I continued to grow
I admit, mistakes I made, I cannot lie
Many bad decisions also, I cannot deny
I wanted to be liked, so I got with the wrong crowd
Did drinking and drugs, of which I am not proud
But, God never left me, He was always near
Saying, "when you are ready, I am here"
I came bad to God, He showed me my new life
He forgave my sins, lifted my burdens and all my strife
He showed me what it takes
To recognize true friends, not a lot of fakes
Yes, God brought me back to reality
Back to my real friends and my family
He watched me as I stumbled, trying to grow
Holding my hand, He never would let go
God, you never judged me or put me on trial
You opened your arms, saying, "welcome home my child"

Marlene Wheeler Scott

What is a Friend???

What is a friend supposed to be?
Is it someone who is supposed to take care of me?
Or is it someone who is there for me when I need to talk?
Or maybe, just have lunch and go for a walk?
Be there to listen to all my gripes and complaints
Make sure I do not lose my patience and keep my restraint
Trying to understand and calm me when I get mad
Or just leave, telling others you were a friend I once had
Well, a friend is not a burner than can be turned off and on
To be used, then tossed aside when you are done
They cannot say they are your friend today
Then tomorrow, just brush you aside, push you away
But then, others too get tired of being used
But then come right back, saying I needed you
I want to be your friend, no matter what
All the past, I have forgave and forgot
I am your friend, no matter what you say
I will be there for you, on any given day
But, that does not mean that I need to go along
With the way you treated me and others, it was wrong
A true friend will stand there beside you
And together, you can see things through
Together, you share the hard times and the good
Just like a good friend should

???????WHAT IS A GOOD FRIEND???????
THEY STAY WITH YOU/BY YOUR SIDE
LISTENING, NEVER ASKING WHY
THERE TO ALWAYS HELP EACH OTHER
SHE IS MY SISTER...HE IS MY BROTHER
TWO OF THESE FRIENDS I THINK
ARE REALLY AWESOME
MY FRIENDS, LINDA AND DAVE CLAWSON

WINTER

Winter is the season that shows us all
What can and does come, after the FALL
Though it brings with it lots of snow and cold weather
It has a 'cozy' way of bringing us together
It brings in the snow, blanketing the earth
While also covering vegetation that will again give birth
Yes, God divided time into four seasons
And for every season, He had a purpose, a reason
Spring brings forth the gentle rain
Letting the flowers and trees begin to bloom again
then comes the Summer, the birds are chirping and singing
Vacations and family times it is now bringing
Then Fall comes, these tall and graceful trees
Will soon color the earth with their beautiful leaves
Winter is the favorite of so many of us
It slows us down, saying, no need to rush
Sometimes is tends to shut us all in, no place to go
Yep, now, it is time to start shoveling the snow
Then, the Sun will come, melting it all away
Leaving us all with memories of Winter's Snow covered days

Your Wedding Day

Congratulations to my beautiful granddaughter Keri
Who, on this day, Phillip, the man of her dreams, she will marry
A beautiful bride I know that she will be
Walking down the aisle on the long awaited ceremony
Friends and family have come from far away
To share and be with you, on this, your special day
I wish that we could have also been there
But, know that we love you and that we care
Marnaw and Papaw keep you always deep within our heart
Today, we send to you our love, as a new day now you will start
The love and the trust between the two of you
Is sealed today when before God, to each other you say, I DO

Congratulations ....Keri and Phillip
Forever....Mr. & Mrs. Phillip Golding
Remembered........... August 09, 2014

ZACHARY

I know that it has been almost a year
Since I left the family that I loved so dear
But, God did not say that you should put aside
Memories of a loved one who has "died"
But that we should hold them forever in our heart
Go on with our lives, each generation becomes a new start
You must take care of yourself and each other, this to you I say
Though I have moved on, God has given to you another day
Son, I want you to take pride in all that you do
Because the way you live your life will always reflect on you
Zachary, not only were you my son, you were also my best friend
Always there for me when needed, embracing me right up to the end
Son, I want you to stand firm in all that you do and believe
So that one day, God's promise to you, you will one day receive
We can still have talks, in spirit to man, but one on one
I will hear you and we in that moment we
will again be like Father/Son

ZACHARY
YOUR FATHER LOVED YOU VERY MUCH AND THOUGH THE PAIN
FOR YOU OF SEEING YOUR FATHER FOR THE LAST TIME, HOLDING
HIM WILL FOREVER BE A PART OF YOUR MEMORY, YOUR FATHER
SAYS YOU MUST LET IT GO AND KNOW THAT IT GAVE HIM COMFORT
IN KNOWING THAT YOU WERE THERE, AND HE DID KNOW...
THE HEART AND MIND ARE A COMPLEX THING AND IT CAN HELP
US OR BREAK US WE CANNOT DWELL ON THE PAST BUT MOVE
FORWARD, WORK FOR THE FUTURE OF YOURSELF, YOUR FAMILY,
THE NEXT GENERATION...LET OUR LOVED ONES BE PROUD OF US...
LET THE NEXT GENERATION BE ONE THAT WILL HAVE MEMORIES
OF LOVE...IT IS THEN THAT WE KNOW WE MADE IT GOD BLESS

God Inspired The Best in Me